Paul + Rosie

A VAGABOND IN FRANCE

Paul Williams
Illustrated by Rosie Williams

W0009974

MINSTER PUBLISHING

Published by Minster Publishing
www.avagabondinfrance.com

Copyright © Paul Williams 2008

Paul Williams asserts the moral right to
be identified as the author of this work

Illustrations, line drawings
© Rosie Williams

Cover design © PFA Williams

ISBN: 978-0-9558356-0-5

All profits from the sale of this book will be donated to the
Parkinson's Disease Society.

For Rosie
who would have loved to come
every step of
the way

Now that he had utterly wrecked his reason he fell into the strangest fancy that ever a madman had in the whole world. He thought it fit and proper, both in order to increase his renown and to serve the state, to turn knight errant and travel through the world...

Cervantes, *Don Quixote*

... every day is a journey, and the journey itself is home. From the earliest times there have always been some who have perished along the road. Still I have always been drawn by windblown clouds into dreams of a lifetime of wandering.

Matsuo Basho, *Narrow Road to the Interior*

Roving has always been, and still is, my ruling passion, the joy of my heart, the very sunshine of my existence.

R.M. Ballantyne, *The Coral Island*

LONDON

Winchester
Bishop's Waltham
Portsmouth

St. Malo

PARIS

Bois Mandé
Hédé
Rennes
La Couyère
Châteaubriant
St. Mars la Jaille
Ancenis
Beaupréau
St. Laurent sur Sèvre
Réaumur
Foussais-Payré
Niort
Aulnay
Matha
Jarnac
Châteauneuf sur Charente
Lerse
Festalemps
BORDEAUX
St. Laurent des Hommes
Le Fleix
Eymet
Puymiclan
Clairac
Bruch
Francescas
St. Puy
Condom
TOULOUSE

0   100 km

viii

Contents

FOREWORD

I heard the car before I saw it, a rusty old Renault 5, screaming along in second gear coming unsteadily round the bend. I saw the two unshaven faces jerk up and smile when they saw me jump on to the verge, then the man's bare arm out of the window and a shiny black pistol pointed right at my head with a narrowed eye taking aim along the length of his arm, keeping me in his sights as they careered past. In that split second I glimpsed the glint of sun on the barrel a foot away from me, the finger round the trigger, and for just one moment I thought I might die. I would never have embarked on this walk if I had known that someone would pull a gun on me.

This is the most terrifying memory I have. The rest, just as moving though less melodramatic, burrowed into my subconscious and emerged some weeks later in the shape of this collection of anecdotes and experiences as I walked through France from top to bottom. Rambling thoughts in the true sense of the word.

It all started in autumn 2006 when I walked from my house in Winchester, England, where I have lived and taught for 27 years, to my house in St. Puy, S.W. France, a journey of nearly 500 miles. It was an idea I had been nurturing for years but it seemed particularly fitting that I should start then having reached 60 in July and with the celebration of our 25 years in St. Puy coming up in August. Put quite simply, I walked from Winchester to Portsmouth, then from St. Malo (where the ferry docks) to three kilometres beyond St. Puy, in the heart of the Gers, at the top of the little valley where our house is.

Proust thought that incorporating too much intellectual analysis into a work was 'grande indélicatesse'. I hope I have avoided 'great indelicacy' here by endeavouring to describe what I saw, not what I think people expect me to have seen. Some of my observations run counter to what most people know and think about France and the French way of doing things. I hope I am shedding some light on the changes that are taking place in a France that is no longer what it used to be just a few years ago.

Before setting out I keenly looked forward to early starts at first light under a cloudless sky, savouring the *plat du jour* in a village bar or, failing that, having *baguette* and *saucisson* sitting on a well-located smooth dry stone overlooking an unequalled view, finishing my day's walk at around 3pm, a short siesta on a comfy bed, a fabulous, cheap and early dinner prepared and served by a rosy-cheeked *paysanne*, followed by the deep uninterrupted sleep of the Just. In more lucid moments, however, I knew I would have few days like that. Things would go wrong. I would miss my way. Despite record drought levels in summer 2006 it was probably going to rain and thunder in September and October. Dinner might well be occasionally disappointing or no more than damp *baguette* left-overs and I would be paying plenty of good money for not very comfortable accommodation. I feared my walk might not be entirely as I had planned and that this journal might turn into a catalogue of woes.

1

The Itchen to the Channel

Winchester to Portsmouth, the first part of my walk, should take just two days and I can save money on accommodation by catching a bus or train back to Winchester after the first day's march and spending the night at home. I have heard of a new footpath known as the Hampshire Millennium Pilgrims' Trail that goes from Winchester to Portsmouth, then on to Mont St. Michel via St. Malo in France. For £2-50 I can buy an enticingly-packaged Pilgrims' Trail pack held together by distressed red string wrapped round a blue paper button. The pack and the documents within are of a suitably antique parchment shade and each document is made to look like a facsimile of something much older. The one called Pilgrims' Record, for example, starts with an illuminated 'P' and informs me that such a record 'was used as proof of their pilgrim status and to provide a log of their pilgrimage'. There are four spaces for rubber stamps: Winchester Cathedral; Bishop's Waltham Palace; Portsmouth (a choice between the Port Manager's Enquiry Office, or the Tourism Manager at Portsmouth County Council); The English Channel (which means the information desk on board any Portsmouth ferry destined for St. Malo). On the front of the record is a neat line of cockle shells and a modern picture in the medieval style of pilgrims arriving at Mont St. Michel either on horseback (rich pilgrims) or on foot complete with a bag and a stake to assist walking (poor pilgrims). Given prominence in the foreground is the ubiquitous barking dog, a phenomenon that the long-distance walker becomes very familiar with. In the background is a primitive representation of Mont St. Michel optimistically guarded by a single soldier with a hatchet. A dove flies over the highest tower holding an olive branch in its beak.

The trail map is just as charming with houses and trees drawn on it to depict villages and woodland, a recumbent pilgrim eating and drinking from a flask to depict a pub. Another pilgrim, looking lost, shades his eyes and searches for the path, whilst local peasants scythe, sow and plough in a bizarre mingling of the seasons. Even more extraordinary is the giraffe standing on the road that passes Marwell Zoo. The trail itself is a series of red dots and there is an accompanying text that seems to give all the necessary instructions.

Armed with the Pilgrim's Record I make my way to the Cathedral which is only a hundred yards from my front door, my mind racing with thoughts about the long journey ahead to the south of France. I am lucky for it is one of those days when the nave has been completely cleared of furniture so I have an uninterrupted view from the West Door right up to the Rood Screen and beyond of the longest Gothic nave in the world. I walk the length of the nave round one side of the choir past the high altar and pause for a moment before the statue of Joan of Arc, burnt three times in 1431 at the age of nineteen because her organs survived the first two attempts. She stands just a few metres from the tomb of her tormentor Cardinal Beaufort who ordered the burnings. Her famous injunction to 'bouter les Anglais hors de France' (kick the English out of France) is still remembered so I need above all to make my peace with her before embarking on my long walk. In order to get my Pilgrim's Record stamped I have to go to the Vergers' Vestry on the south side, a large and impressive room which I have never noticed before. I am told that this is an unusual request but the rubber stamp is produced and thus my long walk to St. Puy officially begins. I am intrigued to discover that the stamp spells the word Vergers' with an 'i', and so does the sign on the door, a spelling peculiar to the Cathedral which I learn today for the first time despite having lived here for nearly thirty years.

I am already very familiar with the walk as far as Owslebury (Black Birds' Fort, hence the two ravens hovering on the trail map), passing on my right the pretty bridlepath flanked by high hedges and clumps of hawthorn with handsome horses in the fields behind leading to Twyford. I assume the walk will continue to be straightforward beyond the delightful Owslebury church because my trail map makes it sound so, but sadly it isn't and I soon get hopelessly lost. I feel a bit foolish now because this is home territory and I should be able to combine many years' walking experience in this area with the somewhat sparse information on the trail map to make sure I find the right path. Moreover, the sky is threatening so I can't even be guided by the sun, nor have I brought a compass. Looking on the bright side, I am pleased that these problems have presented themselves on the very first day and I welcome the steep learning curve.

At this very early stage therefore, I am obliged to resort to asking for directions. I walk down a very busy road full of early morning traffic and knock at the glass door of a smart modern house with polished stone balls dotted around the drive and speak to a very agreeable and attractive young housewife who is not at all perturbed by this odd stranger on the doorstep. On the contrary, the door is flung open and all defences lowered. She scrutinises the map, says it looks rather poor to her, then directs me very precisely and intelligently to the correct path which turns out to be well signed all the way to Bishop's Waltham. The countryside along the way, however, is hardly attractive. The path follows some pylons which hum menacingly and pass very close to a large housing estate, then it leads me to the banks of a stream which, at first sight seems delightful but has a notice on the bank which says: 'Stay away from the water: oil'. The cows on the opposite bank, however, pay no attention to this and drink their fill. The water remains distinctly oily until I abandon the stream on the outskirts of Bishop's Waltham.

I know that my bus back to Winchester leaves in about ten minutes and, since there is only one every hour, I must waste no time getting to the centre. I cross the road walking very fast and ask a young mother with a push chair if she can tell me the most direct way. In reply I get hostile silence and a 'don't-steal-my-baby' look as she puts herself between me and the pushchair and begins to walk fast herself. I apologise for any alarm I may have caused her and ask if she could possibly reply with a simple gesture in the direction of the town centre, but she scowls and quickens her pace. By some fluke I reach the bus just on time and sit in the front seat upstairs reflecting on the female instinct to protect her young. To be fair, the local newspapers are full of a story about a stalker who has been terrorising women in the depths of rural Hampshire and the advice is to walk fast and say nothing. My young mother is probably making a statement to the Police as I am whisked back to Winchester with branches loudly scraping the upper deck windows.

This evening is the last at home with Rosie for some weeks. Neither of us is much looking forward to this prolonged period of separation. We can count on the fingers of one hand the number of nights we have spent apart in the last thirty five years and we spend the evening trying to cheer each other up. Once in France I shall be walking almost exclusively on roads and this understandably worries us both. Of course I shall choose the narrowest of roads but there will be plenty of occasions when I shall have to risk the traffic and take the most direct route. There is the possibility of muggings too and the danger of attacks by vicious dogs.

We daren't mention all this, however, and occupy our minds by checking that I haven't forgotten anything and arranging the best times to speak to each other on the telephone. Five weeks doesn't sound too long to be apart but now that my departure date for Portsmouth followed by the Channel crossing to St. Malo is so imminent we both feel a bit miserable.

The next morning's 06:57 bus from a deserted Winchester bus station back to Bishop's Waltham is rather like taking a large taxi because it remains empty all the way. The first part of the walk is straightforward and the red dots direct me round the outside of the famous ruins but then the infuriating instructions on my absurd trail map dwindle to virtually nothing and I curse the cloudy sky, having forgotten yet again to bring a compass. I sympathise with the medieval pilgrim on my map standing on a mound searching for the path. A female dog walker tries to help but, despite living in the area, doesn't have a clue. She takes the map and turns it round and round in an attempt to get her bearings but understandably can't make head or tail of it. The red dots seem to be arbitrarily placed so I have to guess which fields to cross and at which angles. If I carry on like this through France I shall be forced to give up very soon.

It is now 10:50 am, 3 hours into my day's walk, and I have more than a wee thirst upon me but the Golden Lion pub in Southwick is still firmly shut. I wait till 11 am killing time by reading a notice on the pub wall that informs me that towards the end of the war this used to be the unofficial mess for officers billeted at Southwick House (since taken over by HMS Dryad) and that Montgomery and Eisenhower often came here for a break after talking tactics before the Normandy landings. The barmaid who worked here in 1944 is still in the village and clearly remembers that while Montgomery stuck religiously to grapefruit juice, Eisenhower drank half pints of the beer brewed in the brewery round the back of the pub. 11 am comes and goes but the pub remains firmly shut.

I speak to a jovial man with a strong Hampshire accent digging his garden who knows the area well, dismisses my map as entirely worthless and a waste of £2-50, and sets me on the right track. I now understand why the instructions are more than useless. The person who wrote them must have done this stretch in two stages, one from Bishop's Waltham heading south, the second stage from Portsmouth heading north. But he doesn't point this out so all his rights are left, and all his lefts right. Maddening, and I have to live with this for quite a few miles.

Having had no joy at the pub I see a caravan serving drinks and fry-ups in a lay-by so I ask for a tea. This is quite an experience. In goes the tea bag followed by the hot water, then he grasps the jug and is about to pour milk into the polystyrene cup when I ask if I can do it myself, being not over-fond of milk. He clicks his tongue and jerks his head back and almost says 'typical', or words to that effect. One of the other customers, a lorry driver, assumes I have had a good night out and am having to walk back to my car. I tell him that in fact I am on my way to Portsmouth for fun and this makes him laugh so much he almost loses his burger. I opt to say nothing about going on to walk through France for fear he does himself an injury. Another customer gets out of a brand new black Mercedes and leaves its music system turned up high as he walks towards us. He is wearing a smart dark suit and unbuttoned white shirt with two heavy gold chains hanging from his neck. He asks for a 'full fry-up' and doesn't say 'hello' or 'good morning' but 'are you all right then' pronounced in three syllables 'yer-right-then'. Stifled sniggers as I walk away.

The parchment 'trail', which I am now having to read backwards, tells me to cross a huge muddy field and take the lane on the other side but twenty minutes later I am dismayed to discover no way out through a thick brambly hedge with hidden barbed wire. Horrible enigma (as an Indian gentleman was overheard to say when his bus took an unexpected diversion). In the end, with muddied bottom and a torn muscle in my back after having conducted a limbo dance movement beneath the lowest wire, I get into the lane and then on to the noisy road that leads down into the outskirts of Portsmouth, along streets with rubbish piled on the pavements and the occasional mattress in a front garden, through the smarter Georgian district where Dickens lived and eventually on to the cycle track towards the ferry port. The track is on a raised causeway with water on both sides and a notice with holes in it (shotgun?) saying 'Keep clear of the water: dangerous algae'.

I go into the City Bar opposite the railway station while waiting for my ferry and for the second time today am the only customer in sight. Everything is sticky in the

City Bar. My boots stick to the pine floor, my trousers to the plastic stool and my sleeve to the bar. As I lift the pint of lager (no real ale here) to my lips, the glass sticks to the bar causing me to spill a large part of its contents and contribute in my own way to the general level of stickiness. It's a shame having to mark my leaving England with a glass of foreign beer.

The next stage is to cross the Channel to St. Malo. I have chosen to go to St. Malo and not Cherbourg because the distance the other side is so much shorter. It is a source of some amusement to me how many people in both countries consider my crossing the Channel to be quite a stumbling block. Many would have me catch a ferry and spend the crossing time walking round and round the deck. They proffer this as a serious suggestion. Others with a heightened sense of humour emit hollow laughs and suggest I might swim across the water. Some even state that I will never be able to say I have walked all the way from Winchester to St. Puy because getting across the Channel requires taking a form of public transport and that is cheating. All I can say is that I neither swim nor walk across and that I do not include the distance from Portsmouth to St. Malo in the total distance walked.

2

La Rance - La Vilaine

This is the long haul: twenty-nine uninterrupted days walking from St. Malo, on the mouth of the river Rance in the north, to St. Puy and the river Gèle in the south. There is a nice symmetry in the names St. Malo and St. Puy which I find encouraging. I do not find encouraging, however, the name of the hotel I have unthinkingly opted for in St. Malo: the Hôtel Quic en Groigne. A kick in the groin is the last thing I want before embarking on a long journey during which I shall be entirely dependent on my very own spindleshanks to cover every metre. Legs and, particularly, feet need to be protected at all costs for I shall be walking on average between 25 and 35 kilometres a day with only three rest days to gather strength. I am nervous. I keep asking myself: will I have the energy to cover each day's march?; can I stand being away from home for more than a month?;

what if my blisters get so bad I have to throw in the towel?; what if it rains all the time? (the weather in St. Puy at the end of August was pretty dreadful); can I stand the loneliness?; am I likely to lose the power of speech and begin to babble softly to myself like a true gentleman of the road? Perhaps a well-aimed kick in the groin is just what I want in order to put this whole crazy idea to bed once and for all. But it's too late now. I have trimmed my backpack down to the bare essentials with one eye firmly on the ultimate weight. Seven and a half kilos (i.e. half grandson William's current weight) is very little and I should be able to manage that although experience shows how even the lightest loads weigh heavily at the end of a long day's walking. Everything I carry is utilitarian and essential for survival in the modern world. Yes, I have my mobile for I won't survive long if I can't keep in touch, and my electric razor, for to be un-smooth of chin would make me feel scruffier than I already do in my easy-to-launder-man-made-fibre-one-size-fits-all clothes.

I eat at a *brasserie*: oysters followed by coley in the most delicious butter sauce with boiled potatoes. It comes to the table with two 8' long chives in the shape of a cross over the plate (as if one is going to suffer). There is a raw redness about people's faces here which I am not used to. No-one looks well or sun-tanned although the summer so far has been a good one with plenty of warmth and sunshine.

Over there, sitting by herself, is a corpulent lady with a complexion like an old pink rubber tyre complete with pressure bulges that wouldn't pass the M.O.T., and she is wearing pink lace and an orange plastic tiara that glints in the soft electric light. I stare at her for a long time scarcely believing my eyes and wondering whether the House white wine is making me start to hallucinate. At the table next to mine is a young couple from Quebec with a very loud four-month old baby called Antoine who fills the restaurant with his cries until his mother produces a bottle which, when popped in his mouth, produces a sudden silence. I need a touch of harsh reality like this to convince me that I am not dreaming about that lady's shocking-pink complexion and orange tiara. No-one else in the restaurant notices her as she eats her way solidly through the six courses of the *menu gastronomique*. This is certainly very amusing but I can't decide whether it's a good omen or not.

Back in my hotel room with its view over a dull concrete wall I fall into a fitful sleep, my head full of worry, and dream of foaming canine muzzles and broad horizons that it takes hours to cross. My waking thought is to check passport and money or did I really leave them in last night's restaurant? My fellow breakfasters in the hotel at 6:30 am are a retired couple well into their seventies who eye me and my shorts suspiciously as I enter the dining room and begin to wolf down as much as I can in order to build up strength. He has the hotel newspaper under his arm and spends his time talking to a non-listening audience, not reading the paper. She is silent, thin and pale and observes me closely as I secrete a banana and gulp down many cups of tea for fear of early dehydration. The conversation between them and the sleepy hotel *patron* begins. The old man is in a joking mood.

'You'll be making your piles of firewood then?', he asks of the *patron* who blinks politely and doesn't respond. 'I said you'll be making your piles of firewood' insists the old man pointing to the front page headline that proclaims a sharp rise in energy prices if the GDF – Suez merger goes through. Then more weak jokes: 'Coffee in a bar will be even dearer than it is now, and it's dear enough as it is, judging by the price of this breakfast [hollow laughter]…the price of a *croque monsieur* will go through the roof too…we'll all be drinking tepid beer like the English [a cheery glance in my direction] and eating raw food at this rate'.

I force myself to ignore the suddenly considerable weight of the backpack as I try to lift it on to my back, then gingerly emerge into the cobbled street tripping up over my sticks as I take my first steps. St. Malo is not a nice town to leave on foot. Once I am out of the old part it goes on and on through countless housing and industrial estates, past chandlers, retail outlets, workshops, outboard motor dealers and, curiously, in the midst of all this, a very flamboyant wigmaker's with *Féminin et Masculin* painted on the front. I note that many of the roundabouts have a sign on them containing the name of the resistance fighter to whom the roundabout is dedicated. The ordinary road signs are far from helpful and the people I ask have no idea how to get on to the small road to Château Malo, but what they do have is the purply red faces that I noticed last night. The redness covers the whole face but stops beneath the chin and doesn't extend to the neck. Are they keen imbibers of local Calvados or is it the chill sea wind that gives them the colour?

At last one old lady tugging a wheeled basket on her way to the shops knows the country lane I am looking for and warns me that, although it is a thin white line on my map, it is now quite a busy road full of smelly lorries on their way to the recycling centre. She was right to warn me. I calculate there is one dustbin lorry every two minutes going in both directions occupying every inch of the road and forcing me on to the verge, and each lorry leaves behind it a heavy and lingering smell of rotten fish. The *Malouins* without a doubt have a very high intake of fish in their daily diet. After a further half an hour of fast walking I reach the impressive recycling centre with its huge 30-metre long revolving drum steadily turning the materials inside and reducing them to a fine compost. There are piles of the stuff in the yard with minute particles of mussel and oyster shells glinting in the bright sunshine. The recycling centre marks the end of the city limits. I left my hotel one and a half hours ago, a total distance of about 9 kilometres, and now finally I am on my twisty road to Château Malo, dodging the early-morning commuter traffic round every bend.

I am surprised by how lovely the countryside is: clumps of woodland and small fields with hedges all around full of birds that fly off into the sunshine at my approach. There is still quite a dense population here in the country with many people working in St. Malo so there has been a lot of new building. Every village has its new housing estate and there is plenty of land with planning permission up for sale on either side of the road. The general style of the new houses is very pleasing: slate roof and white or cream rendered walls but they are crammed together and laid out in the Canadian style with everything open plan and no property boundaries. The older traditional houses are built mainly of stone and are small and manageable, the sort of thing we would call an extended cottage in England. I don't see any big old houses all day.

The churches, many of which are quite old, are all made of local granite which is so hard that the buildings show no signs of weathering, and indeed sometimes give the impression that they are newly constructed. The granite lid of a medieval tomb depicting a couple lying side-by-side is displayed on the outer wall of the church at St. Père, but the lines are still crisp and the figures firmly outlined. Some of the stone crosses I walk past, most of which are no more than one metre high, are clearly very ancient but the passage of time has hardly left a mark for the stone has barely worn at all.

The timing is perfect: 12:30 and there in front of me a level crossing and two restaurants each serving a *Formule de midi*. I go into the one with all the cars parked outside and a cheerful hum of voices coming from within. There is a sudden silence as the diners adjust to my arrival and watch me trying unsuccessfully to prop my sticks up against a chair. When I put my backpack on the same chair it rolls off, and down go my sticks with a clatter for the second time. No doubt I'll get better at this but for the time being I pretend to be totally unfazed.

At the table next to mine are two old couples each well into their eighties. Fortunately they are all a bit deaf and tend to shout which makes it very easy for me to eavesdrop on their conversation. The leader of the pack is a woman, very smartly turned out and very *vieille France* (i.e. old school and crusty) who clearly in her time has had staff for she treats the poor young waitress somewhat peremptorily and calls her *tu*.

'Apporte-nous du pain', she snaps, and then after the bread has been brought, 'apporte de l'eau,' without even a hint of 's'il te plaît'.

The throwaway phrase that peppers her conversation is 'before Mummy's funeral' which makes me assume that Mummy's demise is a recent occurrence. But if this is the case how ancient can Mummy possibly have been with such an elderly daughter? However ancient, she appears to have had all her marbles (or not, depending which way you look at it) for she had, before her demise, given away all her possessions. 'All I got was an ugly dinner service' says Madame Vieille France, 'but I suppose a dinner service is a dinner service, as I said to Alain just before Mummy's funeral'.

Alain grunts his agreement and the others contribute a nod as there is the serious business of having to eat the food. I learn all about the visit, 'just before Mummy's funeral', of the double-glazing salesman who charged an arm and a leg but certainly got rid of the draughts; then the butcher who delivered sub-standard meat 'just before Mummy's funeral' and refused to take it back because she'd cooked it; then the man who read the meter 'just before Mummy's funeral' and told them the house needed re-wiring. Despite holding the floor for so long Madame Vieille France beats them all to it and wipes her platter clean well in advance of the others. Then she starts on young people who nowadays have 'too much leisure and push their babies around in wide push chairs occupying all the pavement, and you should see them eating pastries at all hours too' (this from a woman who has just made vast inroads into the cheeseboard, newly re-stocked by the long-suffering waitress). 'And as for cars in the street, we've never had so many before, have we Alain?'

It is highly ironic that the last item on the lunchtime news that I am half watching through one eye at the other end of the room features a splendid old lady, glass of Calvados in her hand, celebrating her 112th birthday somewhere near where we are. Probably an old friend of Mummy's.

Down go my sticks again with another frightful clatter as I struggle with my backpack, interrupting all the conversations at all the tables. For a moment a hundred eyes are trained on me, fixing me with their gaze.

I have never stayed in a French B&B before and begin to wonder what tonight's will be like. I have taken care to book all my accommodation from St. Malo to my destination which on the one hand gives me peace of mind, but on the other fills me with dread because I have to walk all that distance every day. What if I get so tired I can't make it? I suppose I ought to have emergency rations on me and be prepared to sleep in the odd barn just in case I sprain an ankle or am overtaken by prolonged thunder and lightning. This is one aspect of my walk to which I am not looking forward. I am not good lying on hard ground, and doing what the French call *mes besoins* in the open air fills me with dread. Before setting off I was going to find room in the bag for a small flask of the finest Malt to help me face up to the inevitable periods of extreme discomfort, but discarded the idea in the interest of weight. Something tells me that I will come to regret this decision.

Some B&Bs are very upmarket and tend to be located in large manor houses or *châteaux* where the owners probably have sizeable maintenance bills that need paying. The belief appears to be that you can charge at least double the standard rate if the property is approached by a long private drive, or if you call the rooms 'La Chambre Ouest' and 'La Chambre Bleue' and advertise them as filled with pieces of antique furniture. I have booked to stay in one *château* that has been taking in pilgrims to Santiago since the 12th century and has been the home of the same family throughout that period but the €100 they charge in the 21st century for dinner, bed and breakfast is no doubt way above what their ancestors charged in the past. The sacred rite of hospitality in which the host gives succour to the atoning pilgrim and gains favour with the Lord whilst so doing has sadly disappeared. Well, certainly from my route at least.

Tonight's *chambre d'hôte* is one of two old stone houses facing each other on a narrow road in the middle of the country. I ask an old man in the entrance to a barn which of the two houses I should go to. He says nothing but cocks his head in the right direction and promptly disappears. Soon I am with a slightly dotty Madame who opens what at first sight is a cupboard door in the sitting room then leads me up a twisting stair with very uneven risers to my room under the eaves. The bathroom is even further under the eaves so I have to take my shower kneeling down in order not to bang my head on the sloping ceiling. Outside there is a charming garden bounded on all sides by woodland. One or two narrow streams winding their way past the house trickle into a pond and there are sheep grazing on the banks. As the sun goes down a thin mist rises and all the country noises are stilled.

Madame has never had a walker to stay before and is amazed to learn what I am doing. As she busies herself in the kitchen doing the initial preparations for dinner she asks how can I possibly have the energy to cover so many kilometres day after day; how can my legs and feet last that long?

'C'est pas évident' she says, meaning I am not likely to have the energy, my legs will give way and my feet will be covered in dreadful sores. After all, if I don't mind her saying so, I am no longer in the first bloom of youth. This is just the sort of encouragement I need and I spend an hour or two sitting in the garden, checking my socks that are drying on my window sill and seriously wondering if I am going to get very far. I certainly feel very tired and footsore (today's walk was far too long: 34 kilometres) and I am already worried about covering another long distance tomorrow. My fellow guests whom I meet over dinner are just as encouraging and flatly state that I have no chance of getting as far as Rennes in two days' time and that I shall soon be on a train back to St. Malo followed by a boat to England.

'C'est pas évident', they say, shaking their heads in disbelief.

Eventually they change the subject and tell me they consider their work with underprivileged children in Le Havre fascinating and exciting. She is pregnant with a little girl they are going to call Sofia because the father is a second-generation Bulgarian. There ensues a long chat about names and how parents in immigrant communities in France, wanting to give a French name to a new baby, rely on the Church calendar for inspiration. According to the day on which a child is born he or she is given the name that features for that day in the calendar. Fine if you are born on a day with a decent saint's name; not so fine if you are born on a French national holiday. They know children in Le Havre who were born on July 14th and who are called quite simply Fête Nat (the short form of *Fête Nationale* which figures in the calendar for Bastille Day). I find this hilarious because it even sounds as if it might be Arabic.

We are sitting at a dining table in a small dark room crammed full of knick-knacks some of which, on closer inspection, are old and interesting and would fetch a good price in an antique shop. In the stone fireplace is an illuminated bubbling fish tank with a deer's head hanging over it. The three courses for dinner all include delicious Breton pancakes with different fillings and each time Madame comes into the room with laden plates for us she goes over to the tank, sprinkles some feed into it and coos as the fish all go berserk. When she is out of the room we wonder whether we could ask her for more wine (my fellow-diner the Bulgarian has had more than his fair share of the bottle) or whether, in true landlady style, she might flatly refuse. This is the first time any of us have been in a French *chambre d'hôte* so we don't know the etiquette but in the end, the men decide to play safe and take it no further. Loud laughter ensues when Sofía's mother, who isn't drinking, asks Madame to bring another bottle 'for the men who are too shy to ask'. I am secretly delighted as I need a good measure of Dutch courage after my earlier depressing conversations. We needn't have worried about etiquette because on my bill in the morning is half the cost of an extra bottle.

The architecture now begins to change from the neat little homesteads that abounded near St. Malo to larger farmhouses, all slightly over-restored with new bits stuck on the side. The un-restored working farms are untidy, wretched affairs with rutted tracks going right up to the front doors and very smelly cowsheds nearby that must be immensely muddy and depressing in the winter. The farm-hands keep themselves very much to themselves too and only begrudgingly return my 'bonjour'.

I am getting deeper and deeper into the French countryside although, as I approach Meillac, I am still well within commuting distance of St. Malo. Just on the outskirts of the village I come across a school outing, twenty or so small children in a file with two teachers at each end. I hear one of them whisper to her charges: 'Make sure you say good morning to this man when we're closer' and they all chorus 'Bonjour monsieur' as I fumble for my camera.

Every now and again there is a sign off my road down a track to a *menhir*, or local standing stone, but I daren't go and see it because there is no indication of how far away it is. In the meantime I content myself with looking at the extraordinary number of standing stones carefully positioned in gardens. If they are fake and made of fibreglass then they are very good fakes. They are smooth, pointed at the top, no more than one metre high and stand either in mid-lawn or as the centre piece of a bed with closely-cropped, low-growing plants around the base. Gardens with such *menhirs* in them are neatly tended with manicured yew hedges round the boundary and a pair of smart, freshly-painted white gates at the end of the short drive. Houses that are not lived in by commuters are not well looked after and their gardens tend to be entirely abandoned. One stretch of my way between Québriac and Tinténiac has clusters of white, pink and blue morning glory growing wild into shrubs and trees by the side of the road looking wonderfully lush and exotic in the bright sunlight.

The building style changes again. Now some of the older houses are made of a mixture of mud and gravel with a little straw to bind it together and just by looking at the marks on the walls you can tell how long they took to build. The builders must start by erecting wooden shuttering as long as the proposed wall, about half a metre square, then tipping in the mixture and waiting for it to dry and harden. Then they start again, this time tipping the mixture on to the top of the dry wall. Each layer can still be seen quite clearly today. Slightly superior dwellings begin with a short course of stonework but they are mostly without foundations. Windows hang from oak frames that are just inserted into the mud where required. It is all decidedly primitive and a very poor man's building material but it certainly seems to be very long-lasting if properly looked after and if the rain doesn't get in from above. The modern way of restoring these buildings is to add a layer of lime mix to the outer wall. A hamlet made to look like this can be quite pleasing but the overall effect is still a touch dour. Wooden shutters in this part of France are rare so there is nothing to break up the grey/brown of the stonework and the dull dried mud of the walls. There are no climbing plants either.

I am making good time so I decide to try my luck and follow a sign to a whole group of *menhirs*. The sign doesn't mention how far away they are but, although this is not strictly Astérix and Obélix country (their village is much further west), I feel I should make the effort to see some of the ancient standing stones for which Brittany is famous. As soon as I turn off my road I begin to regret it. The land rises steeply and after three kilometres of hill-climbing in a generally north-eastern direction (i.e. pointing away from my ultimate destination) I have still seen nothing and there is no indication on my map as to where these stones are. It is a silly thing to have done for it puts six kilometres on my day and I am not yet fit enough to make such costly mistakes.

I now join a finely gravelled path, described on the signs as a *piste cyclable,* that skirts the Ile et Rance canal all the way to tonight's *chambre d'hôte* near Hédé. I soon get fed up with the path for my feet kick up the gravel which drops neatly into the top of each boot with the result that I am for ever having to stop and balance precariously on one leg whilst removing the other boot and getting rid of the gravel. I am not helped by the large number of cyclists who whoosh past in both directions, giving me very little berth, stirring the gravel and depositing yet more of it in my boots. I yearn for a tarmac surface again but stick to the path because the house where I am heading is virtually on the canal. The land rises just before Hédé and now every two or three hundred metres along the canal there are locks with pretty cottages facing the water, their names in blue and white enamel above the front doors, flowers cascading from window boxes, the lock-keepers standing on the gates as they busy themselves with the sluices. Some of the cottages advertise honey and home-grown vegetables, and they all have a dog straining at the end of a chain madly barking at the boats bobbing at the moorings.

My hostess this evening doesn't cook but, when I inform her that I have walked further than expected today in a fruitless search for *menhirs*, she offers me a bike to take me the two kilometres to a restaurant in the town. It's a very kind thought but the bike has lain gathering dust in an outbuilding for many years and nothing works very well. As soon as I sit on it the saddle sinks into the frame and since the gear cable has broken I am obliged to stick to first gear. I have to pedal furiously in order to advance just a little and because of the low saddle my knees hit the handlebars. I really would have been much better off walking.

Hédé, perched on top of its hill, is a much sought-after tourist destination being just off the canal with pleasure boats able to go upriver as far as Rennes and beyond. The locals begrudgingly accept all the tourists who flock to their town but they keep themselves very much to themselves and don't speak or smile much at all. There are plenty of houses made entirely of the local dark grey, sometimes black, stone and it is really quite a gloomy place. Local residents have tried to cheer it up by painting the cement between the dark stones white, and the woodwork of the windows and doors in bright blue and yellow colours, but somehow this doesn't work, although a number of people I speak to think Hédé 'très joli'.

A redeeming factor is the ruined *château* which stands on an outcrop of rock on the edge of the town but the local council have not increased the charm by installing a couple of games pitches complete with fencing and goalposts within the ancient walls. These are four to five metres high and three metres wide, and it is just possible to walk on the top along a narrow path with low-growing sedums and alpines on either side. I scramble up and advance as far as I can, picking out in the distance today's walk along the canal but my chronic vertigo soon gets the better of me, not helped by my legs which are trembling after all that frantic pedalling.

Flaubert came here once and declared in his journal how impressed he was with his walk along the tops of the walls which afford a broad view all around. He commented on the white roads cutting through the woodland and complained about one carriage in particular that drove straight past not stopping to allow the occupants to admire this view. He would not have liked the roar of traffic on the new fast road to Rennes below the ruins or the red Ferrari I watch disappearing into the distance with sparks flying out of its exhaust. Although the roads are all asphalted now he would recognise the woodland stretching away to the horizon, and this walk along the top of the walls which must be unchanged since his visit, but he would be dismayed by the pace, bustle and noise that accompany this glorious sunset. As I get to ground level a youth on his motorbike with his girl on the back zooms loudly past me and skids to a halt in a cloud of dust by one of the games pitches. They both have earphones and wires leading into their pockets.

One of the doors in the main square that I went past earlier now has the word 'Bar' written on a plank hanging on a couple of hooks to one side of it. Leaning against the bar inside are three men talking animatedly to the owner who takes no notice of me as I stand waiting to be served. When he finally places my glass of beer in front of me he goes outside, unhooks the sign and props it up against one of the chairs inside. I take my time then order another beer and become engrossed in the local newspaper. I can't imagine how he manages to make any profit for he has only been open for about an hour.

The church, just off the main square, is surrounded by grass, which is unusual for France, and on this grass there are some remarkable sculptures by Jean Boucher, a sculptor who spent his last years and died here in 1939. There is a very moving memorial dedicated to American volunteers: the bronze head of a young man on a stone plinth in the middle of a well-tended bank full of seasonal flowers and small bushes of rosemary for remembrance. Close by is a fine 'Tête du Chemineau' (vagabond's or tramp's head), which sets me thinking. His eyes are fixed firmly on the road ahead and the cut of his jaw beneath a full beard reveals an extraordinary degree of determination. He doesn't have the look of a man who wanders aimlessly from place to place. I can well imagine him as a true traveller, walking for the sake of walking, taking pleasure out of rounding every bend, keen to discover new horizons. I feel some degree of affinity with him.

The Monsieur at my *chambre d'hôte* makes a deeply philosophical comment as I breakfast: 'Ah, marcher, ça se fait, mais il faut le faire quand même'. It is almost impossible to translate but I suppose it would be something like this: 'So you're walking all that way... Some undertaking'. He joins the growing number of people who can't get their heads round the fact that anyone would want to walk such a long way, like Boucher's Chemineau, purely for fun. Pilgrims to Santiago de Compostella belong to an entirely different category in that they are proper *pèlerins* on a *pèlerinage* and one would never refer to them in France merely as walkers, although St. Malo to Santiago is two and a half times the distance I am walking.

This morning's newspaper Ouest France carries a disturbing item about a jogger in the centre of Rennes who was badly beaten up yesterday by a gang of youths.

Apparently they jeered at him, he retaliated with an obscene gesture described amusingly in the newspaper as 'le doigt d'honneur' and subsequently is likely to be in hospital for about a month. I reflect rather gloomily on the fact that a jogger looks much more normal that an ageing walker swinging sticks so I had better watch out. I also wonder who would be better off, the medieval pilgrim fighting off the plague and a cloud of horseflies, or the 21st century walker being mugged by a gang of thugs. I find it impossible to choose between the two.

I have chosen the old D road to Rennes which runs alongside the new fast dual carriageway. My road is coloured white on the map which means that it should have little traffic, but because it always was the main road linking Rennes to the Channel ports it is a much broader road than a narrow rural lane, so the little traffic that it has drives at breakneck speed and I have to remain very alert all day. I think it must be an old Roman road because it is dead straight and very conducive to breaking the speed limit. I don't see any police cars, which implies that all the speed traps are on the new road, so those in the know are well aware of which road to take. The old road is separated from the new by no more than a few hundred metres at its widest point so the background noise level is fairly high all the time. Those that have chosen to live on the old road have the worst of both worlds as they have the constant roar of traffic to the rear and very fast-moving vehicles past their entrances at the front.

One very commendable thing about the old road is that it has real kilometre stones standing one metre high with the torch of liberty standing in relief on the front and 'Voie de la Liberté 1944' written above. It is good to be following in a liberating army's footsteps, although on reflection this road can't have been as broad or as fast in the 1940s and I assume the liberators all advanced in motor vehicles, not on foot. Milestones like these are generally disappearing throughout France and are being replaced by anodyne flat slabs of concrete or plastic posts which do no damage to the driver if his car crashes into them. It will take just one bad accident on this old road for their continued existence to be in jeopardy.

I go past one splendid old farm, a dilapidated well-worn building with shiny black grime where hands have touched the doors and shutters over the ages, a real farmyard full of healthy hens and a good rich smell. There is a woman in carpet slippers and a dressing gown emptying a bucket of swill over the half door of a pig sty. A 2CV and a Diane are dumped next to each other in an adjoining field; another 2CV covered in honourable dents and scratches but still in use is outside the front door.

A bit later, still some way from Rennes, is another old house with a restored façade. As I approach, walking quite fast and swinging my sticks, a little old lady comes round the side in order to go in the front door. She quickens her pace, utters a terrified 'bonjour' in response to mine and scuttles inside locking the door behind her. I can quite clearly hear the key turn.

I am lucky again at lunchtime finding a busy little café offering a *formule* with a set menu for €10. It is always good to sit down after twenty or so kilometres and take my boots off. I try to do this as discreetly as possible so as not to put off my fellow diners but the ones closest to me all notice. It would be less anti-social if I sat at one of the tables outside but I've had my fill of fresh air and solitude and prefer the smoky companionship of indoors.

Unfortunately the food, as happens regularly over the next few weeks, is decidedly disappointing. This is more than adequately compensated for by the young couple who are running the show. I get the impression that they haven't been doing it for long as the place has had a face lift and the notices on the wall have a fresh look about them. One above my table is entitled *Traçabilité des Viandes Bovines* and informs us all that the *entrecôte* is from Brazil (something an English restaurateur would hardly wish to divulge); the *steak hâché* from Spain; and the *bavette* from France.

Our hosts, and you couldn't make it up, are called Laure and Laurent, both in their early twenties, but there the similarities end. Laurent is hyperactive, taking orders and serving 10 people on the terrace outside and 20 inside, running between tables with various dishes perched up his left arm leaving his right free to shake hands as others come and go past him. He is obviously enjoying himself, determined to please his customers and wears a constant broad smile. He must have run quite a few kilometres by the time the last customer leaves. Laure in the meantime works sluggishly behind the bar, putting full plates at one end of the counter, removing dirties from the other, turning meat on the plancha grill and tossing the chips in the fryer. Her mouth is permanently turned down at the ends as if disgusted by the food she is cooking. And well she might be. The lunch they give me: mimosa eggs (a euphemism for cotton wool), and chicken *chasseur* (more euphemisms, this time for top budget battery hen and tinned veg.) weighs heavily upon me as I set out to tackle the last 10 kilometres of my day's walk.

Almost immediately I see a long line of white high rise blocks on the horizon which grow higher and higher as I get closer. The northern outskirts of Rennes are quite horrid. The old road into the city which I have been following all day is now a busy service road to countless zones full of retail outlets housed in bright aluminium buildings that are shamefully ugly with brash signs advertising their wares. I walk for 7 kilometres past shining warehouses with huge car parks in front full of furniture and kitchens and precious little else. Managers in suits and ties sit in glass-fronted offices, lights burning unnecessarily on this bright sunny afternoon. A young couple with two tiny toddlers slide down the bank outside one furniture shop on to the lethal road, dodge cars coming from both directions and manage to cross only to go into another similar shop on the other side of the road. And there are plenty more for them to visit afterwards, advertising on their façades in flashing neon that they will be staying open all weekend.

The utter ugliness of the outskirts of the larger French towns is worrying. It is just as well that the buildings look so flimsy because they will all need to be rebuilt eventually. I cannot imagine another walker in the next century passing along here and seeing any of these roomy hangars still in existence. It would be so much better for the environment and for one's health to have small shops in the centre, small depots here in the outskirts, small unpolluting delivery vehicles and of course more jobs, but retail is driven by profit and the consumer wants to see and touch everything before making his choice. Perhaps the internet will eventually make it possible to do away with all these retail outlets allowing customers to touch and feel and make their choices without having to see everything available in one place.

When I finally reach the city I cross the river Vilaine and make my way to my hotel along the rue de la Soif (Thirst Street), so called because of the number of bars it contains. If I had realised this I would never have opted to sleep anywhere near here for the revelling continued till 5 am. My old friend Michel is waiting for me in front of the Hôtel des Lices (or Lice Hotel as we come to call it) and we go on a tour to rediscover some of the old haunts of our youth. We were last together in Rennes in the early sixties, both teaching in the Ecole St. Vincent de Paul, a highly regarded Catholic secondary boarding school run primarily by priests. The school had been requisitioned during the war as a hospital for the treatment of venereal disease and a notice to this effect was painted in German above the main entrance It was only a few months before I arrived (April 1964) that the German teacher in the school had finally managed to get it removed. It was still very much the story of the moment and the source of many amusing anecdotes among both the pupils and the staff.

My friends at the time were primarily among the *surveillants* or *pions* as they are called in slang. These are young students employed by boarding schools mainly to do work involving supervision. Each *pion* had his own room, some of which were significantly bigger and airier than others. One poor fellow lived in a glass box at the end of an enormous dormitory and of course had no privacy whatsoever. He used to get dressed and undressed in the boys' bathroom to which he had a key. My closest friend, Michel, a budding writer in those days and an occasional contributor to Ouest France, lived in a tiny room under the stairs which he called his *sarcophage* much to the disapproval of the priests who thought he shouldn't joke about death in such a flippant way. I forget how much the *pions* were paid but it was very little and they were always very hard up. As unofficial *assistant d'anglais* with only eight or nine periods a week I earned much more. We all got free board and lodging, cleaning and laundry and there was always masses to eat. Our dining room was separate from the boys' and we were waited on at all meals by ladies in black dresses with little white pinnies.

Our main enemies were *les corbeaux*, a slang word for priests (it literally means 'crows', so called because of the black suits or cassocks they always wore), who taught their subject and raked in every month a proper teacher's salary of which they could (and did) save every cent. They were an arrogant bunch: Père Huet who was my main reason for being there (an acquaintance, hardly a close friend of my father's) taught English and loved everything to do with England. He even had a very English visiting card bearing his full name in the English manner, Christian Hervé Huet, followed by his academic degrees. We started to call him CH$_2$ for this reason. Things may have changed now, particularly in the business world, but at the time such a visiting card was considered very unusual. Michel and I mercilessly discussed the merits and demerits of CH$_2$ over the lunch table with the real Christian Hervé Huet blinking uncomprehendingly at us through his blue/green tinted glasses.

Our great chum among the lay staff was Monsieur Paol Le Menn (a splendidly *breton* name). Of all the oldies he was always on our side and found our many antics absolutely hilarious. He lived in a large room down a long, highly-polished corridor, and had various priests as neighbours on either side. He taught Latin and Greek with distinction but had no real interests apart from music (he played a portable organ in his room), hi-fi equipment and *pétanque* which he played with style and considerable aggression. The latest hi-fi that was available in the sixties was very bulky and contained in polished wooden boxes and his room was a mass of cables and speaker wires linking the various systems together. Again, Michel and I were merciless making childish puns about his 'instruments of reproduction' and his own set of *boules* with which he played *pétanque* every day outside the dining room. We hated it if any of the priests joined us because that meant an end to any ribaldry. I shrink now when I remember how childish all this was but it was a wonderful opportunity to get to grips with French. I learned French rugby songs and sang them lustily late at night in the Café de la Paix, a very well-appointed bar in the centre of town with a smart glassed-in terrace on the pavement. I became quite fluent in French student slang because I spent every spare moment talking, laughing and singing. CH$_2$ took me to one side on the eve of my departure and told me he thought I had wasted my time, but he couldn't have been more wrong.

Michel warns me before we go to visit Paol Le Menn. Alzheimers is beginning to take its toll and has already accounted for much of his long-term memory. He remembers Michel as a recent memory, not as one from the distant past. He wouldn't remember me and I must be prepared for that. We telephone him from the car park and as soon as he leans out of his sixth floor window I recognise him: the alert eyes, the long austere face and a shock of now grey hair combed back from his forehead. All his mannerisms are the same: the imperceptible bow as he greets you, the ready smile revealing teeth that haven't changed, the constant movement of his fingers with the same fingernails, looking polished, very clean and well maintained. He looks me straight in the eye and the twinkle is still there. I mention our games of *boules* and he replies 'So we played *pétanque*?...That's all ancient history.' We ask him to play some Breton ditties on the organ (I remember the instrument from the St. Vincent days) and whole vistas of late evenings in his room light up as he touches the keys. He tells us that he plays *boules* with his left hand and that his first teacher forced him at the age of seven to write and to draw with his right. He reminds me how he can write backwards with his left hand then hold the paper up to a mirror and read what is there. He writes a few words on a piece of paper but then can't find a mirror so we have to work it out for ourselves with a lot of help from him: 'I am very pleased to see you again.' And yet he doesn't really know who we are. Michel's latest book is on the table with a dedicatory note on the front page but he hasn't understood that the Michel before him is the same Michel of the book. He is at his window as we return to the car park and waves and waves until we are out of sight.

We drive past the home where old priests spend their last days, a grand 18th century edifice with a courtyard and high metal gates in front, and I learn that most of the ones I remember are dead, then on to St. Vincent itself. A bit of land has been sold for redevelopment on one side of the main gate but the rest is totally unchanged. Even the bar on the corner where we used to have a pre-prandial *pastis* is still there. Unnerving? No, not really. Just sad to think of all those lives passing by like so much water in a river, lives that had touched and affected me in my youth. One of the priests is now married with a family and lives in Bergerac. My old friends, the *pions*, are in their sixties, either with or without their original wives, and are all dispersed throughout France. And so the river flows on.

Breakfast at the Lice Hotel is so extraordinary that it needs to be recorded. I am the first in the dining room at 6:30 am because I know there is a long walk ahead (35

kms) and I need to get an early start. Also getting out of
Rennes and finding my road (I now have a compass, but
no street plan) might take longer than it should so I want
to have started by 7 am. Waiting for me on the breakfast
table is six inches of *baguette* and a small (not normal-sized)
croissant which I demolish in a matter of seconds. When I
ask for more the very affable young man who is in charge
says that I can't have any because they have allocated equal
portions of bread and *croissants* among all the guests so if I
were to have more someone would go without. I suggest
that he has plenty of time to go and buy more bread for
other guests, that my need is real and immediate and that I
have a very long day's walking ahead of me. But the young
man plays it by the book. When I protest again reminding
him that I am a guest in the hotel and the hotel has a moral
obligation to give its guests breakfast in accordance with
each guest's definition of breakfast (mine being: more, now,
please) he disappears into the kitchen and re-emerges with a
plastic bag containing the previous day's sliced bread which
is leathery, chewy and very unpleasant to eat. He then tells
me I can't pay by cheque and don't I have a Visa card. No, I
lie, determined now to make his life difficult, nor do I have
cash (another lie), so you either take my cheque or nothing
at all. Needless to say, at this point the cheque, magically,
becomes acceptable. I refuse to hand it over until he has
given me a receipt.

My compass comes into its own as I begin to make
my way out of the centre of the city in the direction of
the road to Janzé. Rennes at 7 o'clock on a sunny Sunday

morning is particularly beautiful. With the absence of cars and passers-by, the twisted timber-framed buildings by the hotel and the grander 18th century ones in the centre of town are shown off to their best advantage. I pass through elegant squares still with their fountains playing and bits of litter stuck to the little box hedges surrounding the formal gardens in the middle. A young woman sits on the kerb with her head between her knees; further on, spread-eagled on a stone bench with both hands and feet touching the ground lies a man in a drunken sleep, ugly black stubble showing on his chin. The streets bear the signs of last night's revelry: cans and broken bottles, and at the foot of a proud plane tree a couple of syringes. I walk past the *Café de la Paix* where I spent so many hours in my youth. I used to consider its glass façade very contemporary but this morning it seems almost *fin de siècle* and blends in well with the heavy 19th century municipal buildings nearby. The inside is as I remember it and the memories come in a great flood. The joggers start at about eight o'clock but apart from them the streets remain comparatively empty. Even the *boulangeries* I pass are all closed. It is two hours (12 kilometres) before I am out of the suburban sprawl and well on my road to Janzé singing out loud the bawdy French rugby song about a charming young lady called Charlotte who misbehaves herself badly.

3

La Vilaine – La Loire

Janzé looks big enough on the map to contain more than one restaurant but I haven't allowed for the fact that today is Sunday and everything might be closed, so I advance with an ever-increasing sense of doom. When one is covering many kilometres a day the stomach, sometimes more so than the feet, often becomes the centre of one's existence and the thought of not eating anything hot at lunchtime, having been on the road for 5 hours, is dire indeed.

It is at this low point when I am still some way out of Janzé that the old dented car I mentioned earlier suddenly appears round the bend in front of me, its gearbox screaming, and one of the occupants aims a pistol out of the open window at my head. It is black and shiny but the worn rim round the end of the barrel is silver through use. I note these details because the barrel passes within a foot of my head.

In a moment the car is behind me and I hear the scrunch of gears and the bass thump of the sound system as it lurches off towards Rennes. I stand there shuddering at the thought of the finger that could so easily have squeezed the trigger while beating time to the music. It may well have been a toy gun although it looks real enough in the split second I have to work out what is happening. It quite unnerves me to think how easily I might have been reduced to a crumpled heap on the side of the road by a complete stranger who in just a few minutes from now will be swallowed up by the vast acres of anonymous suburbs that surround the city. No one would be the wiser. I muse gloomily on the fragility of life and seriously wonder whether I am wise to continue all alone, exposed round every bend to drivers and passengers who may look upon me as easy prey.

The very slight benefit of my light breakfast wore off some considerable time ago so I am all the more desperate to eat a hearty lunch in order to raise my spirits. I have to admit that last night's celebratory dinner with Michel, sitting in his garden under a sheet of canvas, with the wine freely flowing, followed by a sleepless night in the rue de la Soif, has left me feeling very tired. The last kilometres to Janzé drag on and on and when I finally get there I am truly famished. I see a sign to a pizza restaurant but it is closed on Sundays. I walk to a *brasserie* with a *plat du jour* scribbled on a blackboard but it's yesterday's *plat* and there is no sign of life. My original fears about lunch prove well founded. Nothing is open apart from a dreary bar in the centre so in I go much looking forward to a sit down and a cold drink.

Who knows, they might even be able to rustle up a quick sandwich.

Astonished silence from the two couples who are well into their sixties and showing all the signs of having a very liquid lunch. I know I look an odd sight with my floppy cricket hat, bright green knee bandage, map holder stuffed down my belt and walking sticks and it isn't long before the questions come thick and fast with the subsequent amazement at what I am doing. All four in quick succession emit a 'C'est pas évident, eh?' This highly versatile phrase defies a neat translation but something along the lines of 'Well I never…You don't say…All that way on foot' would be a reasonable stab at it. Both the women have let things go a few years ago and, as is so often the case, are dressed as if they haven't. So inches of flesh inside tight trousers spill out over the seats of the barstools on which they are perched. The one in pink and white with a complexion and hair colour that puts me in mind of a slice of Mother's Pride tells me we are neighbours because she comes from Boulogne sur Mer (every syllable proudly exaggerated) and is very fond of the English (deep drag on her cigarette). At this point her husband, a diminutive man, mutters what I take to be an obscenity into his beer, although I may have misheard.

'Do you have a wife?' asks Sliced Bread, and when I say yes she looks very crestfallen.

'She's taken quite a shine to you', says the other Madame, the bar lady, letting out a loud piercing laugh.

'Well, I'm afraid that's the way it is', I say.

Sliced Bread now draws herself up and out of her slouch and says:

'Are you saying you don't think I'm attractive?'

My reply, almost worthy of Wodehouse, is along the lines of: 'Madame, in all my long years of observing the female form I am forced to conclude that your beauty is sans pareil', which has the required effect for she immediately resumes the slouch.

Meanwhile the bar lady has made me a dubious-looking ham and cheese sandwich with yesterday's bread. As she puts it in front of me she pokes it and leaving her index finger inside the dent she has made says there is more if I want. Although when I first came in here I could easily have eaten a seven-course meal off a *menu gastronomique*, the sight of the sandwich, and indeed the subsequent taste of it, are enough to quell my hunger. The banter continues later when Madame tries, unsuccessfully, to fill my water bag and splashes chilled water all down her front. Another shriek that makes Sliced Bread splutter and cough, then yet another from behind the scenes as she mops down her vast frame.

'Allez, courage, Monsieur', they all shout as I leave. 'Love to the wife when you see her'.

There is a wonderful two-hectare field full of chickens just opposite my *chambre d'hôte* when I leave this morning. There must be hundreds of them. I am glad to have seen them because apparently Janzé is famous for its poultry. I love the way the French attach so much importance to local produce and how quick they are to award *appellation*

'Are you saying you don't think I'm attractive?'

contrôlée status to quality foods and drinks that become part of the national psyche. I have always rejoiced that the year in my part of rural France is divided not merely into the four obvious seasons, but the pig killing season (December to January) when you make hams and sausages and pâtés, *foie gras* in the cold weather, the asparagus season (March to May), *aillets* (young garlic thinnings) in April, *gariguette* strawberries in June, melons in July, lavender in August, violet-skinned garlic in September, new cloudy wine with chestnuts in October. The list is endless and would clearly have its variants in another country, but it is good to have one's year divided in terms of what is best for the table.

The land is flatter and the fields are bigger now, mainly down to pasture, though despite my being only a day's walk from Châteaubriant, home of what is arguably the best beef in the world, I see precious few cattle. I stop and watch two farmers putting some cows with a bull and separating off all the rest with a long rope. The poor bull looks smaller than they whom he has come to service and has a gentle air about him. He is clearly peckish for he seems much more interested in the grass. If like the rest of us he is to be judged on his results I have a feeling he is going to end up soon enough in a *grillade* just a bit further south. I ask one of the men if the little bull can service all those cows and get the reply 'Ah, il est vachement bien mon taureau,' which is impossible to translate adequately but the juxtaposition of 'vachement' and 'taureau' is priceless. Meanwhile the cows, in frisky mood, are prancing round and round the bull; the bull, still hungry, continues to attack the grass.

A little girl aged about 7 stands at the fence that runs along the road in front of her house with four madly barking dogs careering up and down and almost knocking her over, each desperate to sink their fangs into me. She watches me silently with wide eyes, obviously never before having had such an apparition walk by at a pace and swinging his sticks. I wave but get nothing in return.

I walk to the top of a very gentle slope near Rougé where there is a great stone church with magnificent rose windows all the way round and a steeply-pitched slate roof. At the top of my gentle slope is a cluster of buildings called La Montagne de Rougé. All to do with supply and demand I should think for we are miles from any real mountains.

Châteaubriant is hidden in a valley so you don't see it till you are upon it. It is dominated by a church with a tall steeple of white stone that looks better at night under floodlight. The death knoll is tolling when I arrive in the rain and keeps tolling for at least an hour. In front of the main door to the church is a smart modern hearse in deep burgundy and everyone is in a sombre mood. Most of the restaurants I pass would serve Châteaubriant steak for my dinner but maddeningly only to a minimum of two people. I am very tempted to say I would pay for double rations and take away what I do not eat in a doggie bag for lunch tomorrow. But the weather forecast is bad and I have visions of gulping down the best steak in the world in a wind and rain-swept lay-by with some damp *baguette*. It is better by far, I think, to stuff myself at breakfast tomorrow and then look forward to a good dinner in the evening. All this concentration on food whilst the goodly burghers of Châteaubriant bury their dead.

My hotel sounded lovely in the guide: Hôtel du Pont de St. Jean, but the *pont* is ordinary and the hotel more so. It is a typical *petit hôtel* with an entrance through the bar. Three dogs, one a dalmatian, who appear to live permanently behind the bar separated from the customers by a grille, go completely mad as I arrive wet and dripping from the rain. The animated conversation round a table of dominoes players ceases abruptly and all eyes are trained on me. With great difficulty Madame silences the dogs then shouts upstairs to Irénie: 'Chambre 18, Monsieur Williams'. Irénie arrives. Well, strictly speaking, her legs do as the stair is steep and she isn't prepared to come down any further so I don't see the rest of her until I have climbed up a bit. The legs are a good precursor of what is to come: short, podgy and waxy. That is Irénie in a nutshell. She proudly shows me my room, at least she stands in the corridor and points for it would be very difficult to get two people in there especially with one of them wearing a backpack. Plastic floor, plastic wardrobe, plastic bathroom and a basin so small I hardly have room to wash my socks. The bed is the narrowest I have seen for a long while (it wouldn't have fitted in the room otherwise) and my view is over the open dustbins in the yard at the rear of the hotel where there is a broken gutter pipe dripping noisily on to a plastic sack.

As I go down to the bar for a touch of human warmth after spending the minimum time possible in my bleak room, I notice the two pictures on the stairs and landing. One is of a little boy, the other of a little girl and they are both crying with huge tears glistening on their cheeks. That, plus the rain, plus the funeral, plus the fact it's Monday and most of those restaurants I saw earlier will remain shut, reads like a sample of Flaubert symbolism. Fitting I suppose for the fifth anniversary of 9/11. I've said a prayer for all who were caught up in it; another prayer for the world; and a third for the Muslim extremists who think dying like this is good for their soul.

In the bar downstairs I am regarded suspiciously by old men sitting in front of their glass of *rosé*. More dark clouds have appeared and now it's beginning to rain hard. The weather map in the local paper is dominated by images of black clouds with heavy rain pouring out of them. A group of schoolchildren have just gone by and goaded the dogs into creating a great din. The children appear to do this regularly because they scarper as soon as the frantic barking starts. Madame behind the bar is for ever going 'schh' and 'taisez-vous' for the dogs create every time anybody goes past the open door. There is one restaurant open, a dubious-looking well-lit *brasserie* with plastic menus, where I know I am going to eat badly.

At early breakfast the following morning I notice the five terrapins in the window. They are in an aquarium the size of a school trunk and they must be very old for they are each the size of a dinner plate. I can't imagine how I didn't notice them yesterday. Madame has built a loose brick base which allows them to hoist themselves out of the water and have a few moments on semi-dry land. One of the bricks doesn't sit tightly on the others so every time a terrapin touches it an aqueous thud emerges from the aquarium. They are obviously hungry (I am only too aware of the signs) and my breakfast is accompanied by frantic scramblings on to the brick perch and tortoise necks straining out of the water. There are three commercial travellers with me but they have either been here before or are totally unalert for they seem oblivious to what is going on. After all, it isn't every day one shares a breakfast room with five ravenous reptiles. Every time Madame passes with baskets of bread and trays of coffee the scramblings increase to fever pitch. I desperately want to see what they get for breakfast and my spirits are lifted when she unlocks the cellar door and disappears. What's it to be? Something alive, surely? But she comes back with a plateful of butter. 'Schh' as she passes the tank. 'Schh' again to the dogs who are hungry too.

It's still raining so I get into my bad weather clothes, pay my bill and bid farewell.

'C'est pas évident', she says.

'Eh non. C'est pas évident', I reply delighting in the utter versatility of this expression. 'It looks set in to me so you're going to get wet' would be a rough translation of this one. And she is right. It rains heavily and solidly until midday by which time I have covered 20 kilometres. My expensive weatherproof clothing made with the very latest breathable fabrics doesn't behave in the way in which I think it ought. As I walk I build up quite a steam which means that I end up being just as wet on the inside as on the outside. I don't see much because when it rains heavily I have to keep my head down to stop the rain trickling down my neck, whilst at the same time remaining alert to approaching vehicles which seem to be united in the common purpose of covering me with spray. However, I do notice an abrupt change in the style of houses. Now they are built purely out of slabs of slate bound together with mud. When restored, a light sand render is inserted in between each slate which lightens the overall impression but the slate remains black, even in dry weather, and the general view of the house is dull with its black slate roof dominating all.

I wondered yesterday where all the beef cattle were. Well, they are here, south of Châteaubriant, and they extend as far as St. Mars la Jaille, and there are thousands of them. The fields now are enormous, many hectares each, and they contain large herds which stand forlornly in the mud staring at this odd man moving determinedly south, swinging his sticks and singing Brazilian samba out loud (actually all the Ataulfo Alves songs and particularly *Sei que é covardia* which is one of my favourites), or quite simply talking to himself. I have developed this tendency to sing and talk to myself for there has been little company so far in rural France and I have decided that if I don't talk to myself at regular intervals I will probably lose the power of speech.

There are lots of calf sheds that let out a ghastly stench in which I can detect some of the taste of last night's steak which was horrid and full of gristle (I was right about the *brasserie*). Attached to the sides of the sheds are huge hoppers with a pipe going straight through the wall into the feeding troughs. A notice proudly declares this to be

French veal in the making. So that's all right then. 'Vive la traçabilité'. One field I go past has about 80 head of cattle with tags on their ears that behave like a pack of very excited but very silent dogs behind a fence. As I approach they charge me then swerve round in a huge circle all together and come back to the fence, the only noise being the squelch of their feet in the new mud. I seriously think their tails are wagging and half expect them to bark at any moment. Then they begin jumping up, trying to vault the fence, all this in complete silence. Maybe it is the samba, or my bright green knee bandage, or my forgotten socks dangling like a double tail from my bag that sets them off. Whatever it is, I am sorry to have to leave them looking so forlorn as I continue up the lane.

At St. Sulpice les Landes there is a little bar into which I dive and stand dripping to the astonishment of the young woman behind the bar and a depressed, silent man sitting on a stool. There are only two things on offer: pre-packaged pizza and/or *croque-monsieur*. I need something. I have been walking fast for five hours in energy-sapping conditions so I order a *croque-monsieur* and immediately regret it. It is difficult to imagine food tasting so horrible and looking so unappetising, and it is depressing to see a young energetic woman in charge who doesn't seem to care. I so miss the France that I remember from my youth where places like this would have had a *plat du jour* of memorable deliciousness and a nice jovial lady serving it. I recollect one ivy-clad establishment in a tiny village not unlike this one where we stopped when I was a small boy. The delicious

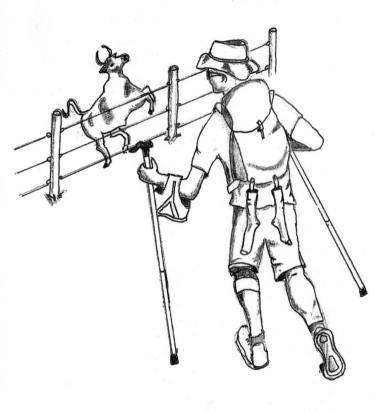

Maybe it is the samba, or my bright green knee bandage, or my forgotten socks dangling like a double tail from my bag that sets them off.

cooking smells assailed our nostrils as we sat down at a table with starched linen, fresh flowers and polished glasses. I remember vividly my mother's sharp intake of breath and the puckered, disapproving mouth of the lady in the corner when I knocked over my glass. All the copper and brass pipes in the lavatories where I retreated to smarten myself up were so highly polished I could see my face in them. When I got back to the dining room the disapproving lady was scratching her head with her fork and my mother and father were both trying hard not to laugh.

Where I am staying tonight at St. Mars la Jaille is just my kind of hotel, a *petit hôtel*, of the best sort. The French understand perfectly well what a *petit hôtel* is and what to expect from it. It is about the same price as a Bed and Breakfast, entirely simple with no flamboyant gravelled drive, usually in the centre of town, and often family run. If the family are involved then French employment law which is heavily biased in favour of the employee can be by-passed quite legally and prices kept as low as possible. So one often sees Granny washing up in the kitchen or a teenager serving in the restaurant for a bit of extra pocket money. Madame or Monsieur probably share the cooking and reception so there is no need to employ a chef. It makes excellent sense and everyone gains.

The entrance to the Hôtel du Commerce is through the bar which has little tables and chairs that extend into the restaurant area at one end. The bedrooms are at the other end, through a door and up some lino stairs. Everything is simple, clean (though not spotless), and proprietress Chantal is cheery, presides over the bar and takes an active part in all the conversations. Here, when people come into the bar, they shake everyone's hand, and again when they leave. A nice touch that, and unusual. As I sit here, the sun has come out (yes, the worst of the day had to be this morning when I was on the road) and there is a steady stream of vintage cars with Tour de France written on them going past the door. There is an amusing man with drink on his breath who says 'Eh putain' every time one goes by and he has now regaled us all with 'Ils sont cons' because they are going all round France. I have decided I will shut up about what I'm doing. How could I explain to such a man my desire to drown like a rat in storms on country roads that lead south? The man who has just come in has said they have started the wine harvest. I'll celebrate that with some Gamay over dinner. Yesterday's and today's horoscopes in the two copies of Presse Océan on the bar cheer me up after my long day's struggle against the elements: 'You will press ahead and achieve your ambition' and 'Difficulties will only reinforce your desire to achieve your objective'. By now Chantal has told the drunk what and who I am so I am obliged to come clean and reveal all.

'Eh chapeau' (great) says the tipsy one and shakes my hand. 'Eh chapeau…Eh chapeau…Eh chapeau…Eh chapeau…'. And then he comes out with the very touching 'I will pray for you'.

His companion, a man who goes to great pains to tell me he is 51 and who has been accompanying his friend drink for drink, shakes his head and says 'Vous allez vous faire braquer…C'est pas évident' , which roughly translated would be I suppose: 'You're going to get mugged, that's for sure'.

Chantal agrees and says I must let her know when I arrive safely at my destination. She has never had anyone quite like me stay overnight before and she has spent a lifetime here. I take a photo of the outside of the hotel looking into the bar. My tipsy friend says: 'Send that photo here with your name, address and 'phone number on the back and I'll get in touch and invite you and your wife to stay. Come and see my 12 day-old son. I've got grandchildren you know but now I've started making children of my own again'.

Dinner is garlic (the first since St. Malo) with seafood and steak all made by Chantal's husband, a very young man whom I had originally taken to be her son. At breakfast Chantal is in a frisky mood perhaps inspired by all my sporting gear.

'Good morning…'Ow are you…good?', all in English. She asks more questions, tells me she is going to be sixty in November, that she has no children but will be celebrating with friends. When she learns I have taught Spanish she practises her 'Buenos días…tienes hambre' with a strong French 'r'. She has already laid the tables in the restaurant behind us, rolling up the napkins into long 18 inch sausages and sticking them upright in the glasses. In the background the radio plays Robbie Williams, then an item on summer book best sellers (this sort of thing would only happen on a popular station in France), then the weather forecast. 'Storms approaching from the Atlantic' she repeats with great concern for me. 'C'est pas évident'. I take a photo of her behind the bar. 'People don't come here any more' she says with a long face. They all want to go to the coast and they take the motorways so we get precious few people staying nowadays. You're quite an exception'.

It takes me four hours to walk the 23 kilometres to Ancenis. At first the country is similar to yesterday's then suddenly it becomes hillier and some of the hills very steep to climb. The houses, however, remain the same: small, mean dwellings, neatly done up and lived in by people who read all the latest Interior Decoration mags. I pass a wide range of highly-coloured drapes over windows, blinds that double up as shutters, and different shaded gravels on the drives. All the time the land is rising, rising until I get to the top of the last ridge some 5 kilometres from Ancenis. There are wide views on either side and straight ahead where the land rises again, but still no river. A number of farm buildings have Roman tiles on them which somehow look wrong amid all the grey black slate. I embark on another long climb and even when I get to Ancenis itself the land continues to rise up a long upward incline, which is odd for I was expecting a gentle slope down to the Loire. In fact, I can't see the Loire until I am upon it because the lie of the land doesn't allow it. The approach to the town is dominated by a large industrial estate with very large, tall buildings. The tallest is the Dairy out of which comes a loud mechanical hum. I assume this is where all those milk lorries I have been dodging have been heading for over the last couple of days.

Then, after a good kilometre, I arrive at the cemetery which often in France paradoxically means you are approaching a lively part of town. Just opposite the main entrance (and it is important enough to have been signposted some time ago) is the 'Funerarium'. I am intrigued as to what this might turn out to be but it is no more than a waiting room with a very large shop attached. Display windows overlook the cemetery filled with examples of plaques that can be bought for the loved-one's gravestone. Above the door is a huge blue plastic butterfly no doubt symbolising the flitting away of the spirit. Here are some examples of what you can buy, enriched with a dedication of your choice: a couple of geese flying in front of a tree, no doubt with Heaven as their ultimate destination, all in imitation brass (an irreverent thought strikes me at this moment: a passing local might think they could easily be brought down to earth again and force-fed for *foie gras*); a bird (another flutterer but species unidentifiable) hovering around an old-fashioned hand water pump (I'm not at all sure what the pump symbolises); and then (this is the best), a whole farmyard complete with pigs, hens, ducks, geese, hayrick and ladder (chocolate-box hayricks need ladders for total authenticity), and a picturesque farmhouse (without a TV aerial or satellite dish despite the fact they have all got them) all stamped on a piece of imitation brass in the shape of a waxing moon. One is really spoilt for choice.

A few metres beyond, overlooking the ring road, and strategically placed at the entrance to the road that leads to the cemetery, is a huge stone crucifix with 'Spes Unica' written on the base. A stone flower vase with holes in the top lies empty on its side. I must be the only person in Ancenis today who has stood and looked at this shrine for a moment or two for the traffic roaring past is only intent on speed. There are hundreds of crosses like this all over France and no-one pays much attention to them apart from the solitary walker who has the time to comment and reflect.

It is now 14 September, my first day off since I started, and I am much looking forward to it. I feel very grand talking of a *jour de repos* because it makes me feel as though I were in the *Tour de France*. It happens to be Thursday and fortunately for me it's market day in Ancenis. The main food market is in a handsome building in the centre of town with all the familiar produce for sale displayed in the usual enticing French manner. I am particularly impressed by the fish which glistens, bright-eyed, on freshly ground ice and doesn't smell at all. There are some fresh water varieties I don't recognise. I ate *anguilles* (eels from the Loire with origins as far away as the Sargasso Sea) last night and am pleased to be able to see what they look like on the slab. The babies are pink and about 8 inches long, the grown-ups greenish and about 3 feet. On the same slab, curiously, are glistening white frog-leg kebabs which look particularly meaty and delicious, all ready for the barbecue.

The street market is unusual in one respect: the large number (perhaps 20?) of stalls selling clothes, many of which are Designer and attract a good clientele. I notice later that there is a dearth of good clothes shops in Ancenis so this market is really filling a need. Apart from clothes stalls there are the usual North African and craft stalls smelling of burning incense sticks with one man displaying long, filthy blonde plaits touting for business by playing the didgeree-doo to a small knot of admirers. Couscous and paella are cooking in vast 2-metre diameter pans and there are chickens roasting on electric spits. The food smells are overwhelming and it is some time now since I consumed my single dry, dull *croissant* for breakfast. Maybe, just maybe today, market day, the Restaurant du Marché at one end of the square into which I have dived for a 'beaker full of the warm south' will provide a nourishing market trader style lunch. It is certainly popular enough with traders and their customers all of whom ask, not for a glass, but a *pichet de rosé* and some empty glasses. They then pour it themselves and clink glasses before each sip. A *pichet* lasts some seconds then out they go. The glasses go into a dishwasher with about a five minute programme, but the *pichets*, unwashed and unrinsed, go straight back on the shelf. With such a fast turnover, it's just not worth washing the jug. The market folk have fascinating faces with a lifetime of happiness etched on them. Just outside the window is a stall selling flesh-coloured reinforced underwear for the over-sized woman with a string of very interested ladies doing their utmost not to look very interested.

I am the first to sit down on the dot of midday and five minutes later all the tables are taken by noisy market traders who keep a watchful eye on their stalls and occasionally run outside to deal with a customer. My lunch is excellent and at €11-80 very good value: melon, salads (not all out of a tin for a change), smoked ham for starters; *boeuf bourguignon* and a *pichet* of Gamay. Disappointing bread, but I have come to accept that the bread served with meals in cheap restaurants offering a *plat du jour* is dull and tasteless. This comes as quite a shock because the pre-conceived idea about French bread, both in France as well as in Britain, is that it is delicious all of the time. Not so, I'm afraid.

Most of the *Château d'Ancenis* is in a dreadful and dilapidated state but it could be saved from further decay with just a little spent on it, and immensely improved if they demolished the one or two atrocities, classroom blocks and dormitories, that were put up in the nineteenth century by the Ursulines who opened a school here (since discontinued). There are some wide, uninterrupted views of the Loire from the ramparts which must have remained unchanged for centuries. An old clinker-built barge with its mast lowered is anchored in the middle of the river and there is no sign of any building on the other side. I learn from a municipal notice that in medieval times earthworks were built out from the opposite bank to narrow the channel nearest the *Château* which made it easier for the *Seigneurs d'Ancenis* to levy charges from passing shipping. The bridge is nothing special but big and imposing and has a decided wobble when heavy lorries drive over it. When I cross it tomorrow I leave the Duchy of Brittany and enter France proper. 'Il suffit de passer le pont, c'est tout de suite l'aventure'[1] as Georges Brassens would have it.

---

[1] Just cross the bridge and adventure lies straight ahead.

4

La Loire – La Sèvre Niortaise

The land on the southern side of the Loire behaves as
you might expect and slopes up away from the river. There
is a striking war memorial outside Liré on a hill overlooking
the river bearing the names of French airmen who were
brought down by enemy fire at this spot in 1944. Chiselled
into the stone including the double exclamation mark is:
'Français Souvenez-Vous!!' This memorial puts me in mind
of the one near the bridge in Ancenis commemorating those
who died in the liberation of the town, again in 1944. It
could well have been the same offensive claiming the lives
of men in the final year of the War who almost made it
home to their wives and families. I have been struck by
the number of plaques erected in churches and in roadside
shrines simply inscribed 'Merci 1944' almost certainly by

survivors or their worrying wives, and I continue to see them right the way through France.

I have walked past literally dozens of *calvaires* (simple crosses) at crossroads, some with a niche in the base containing a statue of the Virgin, usually Our Lady of Lourdes dressed in white and sky blue to whom there is a great devotion throughout the country. Sometimes the grotto where the Virgin appeared to Bernadette is reproduced in miniature, made of slabs of stone with ferns and alpines growing in the cracks. The grander ones have a metal gate, specially constructed niches for candles and a statue of Bernadette kneeling in front of the Virgin. They must have been a constant reminder to travellers in a slower, quieter age to go with God every step of the way, but now cars speed past, their occupants smoking, conversations dominated by the thump thump of the bass drum on the sound system.

Two days ago Ouest France reported a sermon by the Pope visiting his home town in Germany in which he lamented the secularisation of the modern world. In the part of France through which I have walked so far there is little sign of life in or around the churches, many of which are locked. A number of parishes share the same priest and many churches seem to have just one Mass every few weeks. I haven't yet seen a single priest, although I know that nowadays priests are dressed like everybody else so I may have missed them. I may be over-simplifying the problem but I know the majority of people who would still call themselves Catholic never attend services and are ignorant of the Church and the work it does despite the numerous reminders everywhere, the crosses, crucifixes and little shrines which seem to be just quaint indications of how and what people used to believe. On the outskirts of Villeneuve today, two kilometres from Le Fief Sauvin, a huge crucifix standing many metres high is obscured from view by cypress trees planted too close to it with no beaten path and zero maintenance. I almost walk right past without noticing it. And yet there are occasional signs of life. The church of Villeneuve and one or two others I pass today display a big poster outside with the caption *Espérance de l'Eglise* featuring the four members of a model iconic family in vivid technicolour, each smiling beatifically.

In the middle of the driving rain I see a *tabac/bar* and go inside. There is a forlorn-looking old man at a table watching the TV and a bright young couple behind the bar with not much to do. They have the usual reaction to my walk: 'Why on earth are you doing it?' Then she notices my bag. 'Is that all you're carrying?' She is one of those people who would need a whole suitcase as an overnight bag. Then they both begin to calculate, without any input from me, how much the whole journey is costing: so many nights at so much per night; then there's food on top of that; then stops like this one for a hot drink. When they reach the final figure, which is pretty accurate, they sigh, say I am very fortunate, and carry on busying themselves over not much in particular, talking all the while about how they might be able to get out of this rut. They are clearly struggling in a tiny village keeping body and soul together selling lottery tickets, cigarettes and running a bar, and would love to be doing something more exciting and rewarding. It is easy enough for me, I know, to say that they actually have all they need to make a go of this bar and turn it into a good little money spinner. There are precious few bars around as it is, and a good one could be very successful. My tea is served in the latest Italian design orange cup and saucer. With one push of a button she can switch the TV from French soap to the weather channel which reveals in some detail where the bad weather is going to be over the next week and is definitely not good viewing for me. I spend the rest of my morning dodging the spray from passing traffic and thinking how many people I have come across in more depressed corners of the globe who own nothing, live from hand to mouth every single day and who would consider a life like the French couple's entirely unattainable. It's all so relative.

Charming people run the Hôtel de France in Beaupréau but it is obvious from the start that they are strapped for cash. There are a couple of armchairs, a TV and a coffee table in a corner of the dining room which seems to double up as the family room. As I eat my lunch at a proper table the owners' two children back from school sit with a plate on their lap watching the lunchtime news while their mother is fully engaged looking after the guests in the dining room. The décor is tired, each table being separated from the other by a wicker screen interwoven with dusty plastic leaves and flowers. What used to be the way through to the stairs was purloined some time ago for extra dining space and this means that overnight guests now have to use a service corridor that at one point encroaches on the kitchen to get to the stairs.

The building needs considerable structural work and a complete refit to bring it up to today's standards. Both the stairs and the bedroom floors slope alarmingly and there is depressing, kinked and well-worn lino everywhere. My bedroom furniture consists of a couple of wrought iron bar stools and a tall glass-top table such as one would see in a station buffet. The shower and loo are behind a crude screen. The hotel clearly isn't generating enough income to plough some back into the fabric and Madame laments that since the motorways were built few businessmen and very few proper tourists come to this part of France because 'there's nothing to do or see round here'. She is also worried about the 35 hour week and the long term future for her children. Young people in particular are a cause for concern because the new labour laws generate a culture where too much emphasis is laid on the right to work and not enough on cultivating a sense of responsibility. She employs one lady for 17 ½ hours per week who doubles up as chambermaid and waitress. Before the motorways this hotel had a staff of six and the building of a new hotel on the outskirts of town hasn't helped. When I ask for some soap I am told there is none. Five minutes later there's a knock at my door: would Monsieur mind having this soap that has already been used by a previous guest? It is all there is until the delivery tomorrow. Sorry.

I spend hours at my window willing the driving rain to stop and watching the traffic splash its way round the mini roundabout beneath me. When at last it eases I emerge into the wet streets wearing my flip-flops and actually enjoy the sensation of cold drops of rain falling on tired, swollen feet. Madame was quite right: there's not much to see here apart from a handsome stone-built house down a side street with an abandoned tower tagged on to one corner. I reject one smoke-filled narrow bar with *Le Maillon Faible* (The Weakest Link) booming from the television at the far end, and choose another with tall mirrors up to the ceiling covered with posters and white writing advertising what is on offer. One table is taken by local sixth formers from the *Lycée* swapping notes, scribbling homework and sharing cans of Coca Cola. I wonder what a similar group of youngsters would be drinking in England. The weather has dampened everyone's spirits so no-one talks much, and somebody else has got to the paper before me.

I thought the *boulanger artisan* opposite the hotel would provide a good breakfast loaf and *croissant*, but the title is a misnomer for the word *artisan* is just tagged on to *boulanger* for effect. It is not only my poor breakfast that makes me glad to be leaving Maine et Loire by the end of today. There is a distinctly depressed feel to the place and I suspect there is a lot of unemployment. Houses are small and mean. Even the brand new ones don't look solidly built and gardens are left untended. The countryside is scrappy with plenty of untidy farms surrounded by masses of rubbish and the smell of the cooped-up animals is dreadful. I am more aware than most that it has been grey and damp for the last two days and that this may well have affected my judgement but I don't think so.

The centre of St. Philbert en Mauges, however, is strikingly lovely and the village is unusually tidy and well kempt with municipal flowers everywhere and, *chose rare*, a beautifully restored 12th century church which advertises itself as an 'église accueillante' (welcoming church). Most infuriatingly, however, it is shut so I have to make do with the exterior. As soon as I am out of the village standards drop again and the countryside reverts to being untidy and poorly managed.

I suspect the northern and western sides of Cholet through which I pass are the poorer districts. My lunchtime break at La Séguignière is very disappointing indeed and all my fellow diners give the impression of having very few resources. I feel terrible when my newspaper, which I have propped up on a couple of glasses, knocks one of them over. Madame's reaction at first is 'don't worry, that means good luck', but then she goes off muttering 'I'll have to replace the whole set now' which is a bit of an exaggeration as it is a standard glass that one sees everywhere in cheap bars and restaurants, but it is revealing. From the hatch in the wall comes the tell-tale ping of the microwave as each chicken piece with accompanying spoonful of sauce and rice is heated to order. The waitress's 'Bon appétit' rings a bit hollow.

La Séguignière is a disappointment in other respects too. When I rang to enquire where exactly the restaurant was located (long distance walkers worry about exact locations) I had been told that it wasn't 'up' in the village but on the main road 'below'. This led me to believe that it was a hilltop village and might be medieval and rather pleasant. But no. The new smart housing estates of La Séguignière (a Cholet dormitory town) are on the top of the hill, the old village which is crumbling and unattractive is on the slope. The road down is not asphalted but covered in grey gravel and potholed. The centre, just a shop or two and a post office round the church, is, however, quite smart and I take advantage of the postman emptying the box to send my second map home, reducing my burden by 100 grams (long distance walkers worry about grams too).

When my small road crosses the N160 there is a wooden notice on the verge erected by some 1960s green protester in memory of a pond which he calls *l'étang ruiné* that had to go when the new road was built. He clearly still feels very strongly about it because the notice has recently been renewed, each letter carefully picked out with white paint. Le Puy St. Bonnet is a lovely place displaying plenty of civic pride in the care and upkeep of its buildings and monuments, and as I move closer to my hotel at St. Laurent sur Sèvre I notice a gradual change on all sides. The countryside opens up and I can at last see broad horizons from the tops of hills. Farms look more prosperous, the animals better cared for. Houses old and modern are more solidly built, gardens and public spaces more looked after.

The manager of tonight's hotel echoes the sudden change I have seen over the last few kilometres. La Vendée is more prosperous than Maine et Loire and unemployment here is below 5% which is less than half the national average so there is more money available. The recent influx of English people has helped the local economy too for they employ plenty of craftsmen and eat expensively in his restaurant. He has ambitions and is keen to move on and find a hotel of his own to buy in Pyrénées Atlantiques. He is only the manager here and he tells me that the owners have never responded to his suggestions to improve the fabric and expand the clientele. His talk over my *apéritif* suggests to me that he has the necessary drive to do very well when he and his equally competent wife can set up by themselves.

At the entrance to the restaurant is a large glass case with life-size figures within, brightly lit with spotlights depicting a scene from the Vendée uprising (1793 – 1796). It started when the Republican government in Paris decreed that all clerics should swear allegiance to the increasingly anti-clerical National Assembly. The class conflicts that fuelled the Revolution were weaker here in the Vendée where the people continued to maintain strong adherence to the Church, and by extension to the King. The rebels, with their insignia depicting a cross above a heart with the caption *Dieu Le Roi* (God the King), organised themselves into the 'Royal and Catholic Army' and bravely began to fight for their beliefs. When the heroic struggle came to its inevitable end the Republicans under the ruthless Turreau were merciless and practised ethnic cleansing of the most brutal kind. Thousands of prisoners, among whom were 400 children who were seen as future rebels, were tied up in barges that were then scuttled in the Loire. Turreau's orders were simple: 'Exterminate the brigands to the last man'. This genocide at the time was called 'Pacification'.

In the glass case a brave rebel lies dying with his head on a stone pillow, gun and faithful dog by his side, whilst the battle rages all around, but this doesn't seem to put off the diners. The restaurant is busy this evening with twenty or so *chasseurs* (hunters) and their wives, all of whom are dressed so elegantly they make me feel quite out of place in my ghastly one-size-fits-all-man-made-fibre-easy-to-launder trousers and tee shirt. As I leave the restaurant I see the manager lose his temper with one of the staff, push a dish back violently into her hands and then shout an obscenity down the serving hatch. At breakfast professional calm has returned but I am left with second thoughts wondering whether he really does have the required management skills to go far in this business.

I now have to go into the centre of St. Laurent with its magnificent basilica to pick up sandwiches at the *boulangerie* for dinner this evening as the *chambre d'hôte* where I am heading doesn't do meals. I have spoken to the Madame on the 'phone and there is no chance even of a cold collation so I should bring my own food if I wish to eat in the evening. I certainly shall wish to eat, Madame, said I, because I calculate I will have walked 33 kilometres by the time I reach you and will be in need of some refreshment. But this doesn't move her stony heart, hence my trip to the *boulangerie*. My own heart sinks when I see the sandwiches (and pay for them: €12). They look as though they were made last night with soft, spongy rolls, wet salad leaves and tuna, and are wrapped in cling film. It is 7:30 in the morning so they have to survive in my bag for another twelve hours. Dinner this evening will be a sorry affair.

As I leave St. Laurent I go past a smart modern building called the *Centre de Formation et de Promotion des Maisons Familiales Rurales* which I assume to be a sort of Adult Education centre, though here, I suspect, patrons are not expected to pay anything. It seems to be funded by the Department of La Vendée. The older houses that I see now on either side of my road are built of the local granite which is a delicate pinky yellow colour which, although not as warm as the stone further south in the Gers, is a significant improvement on what I have seen since St. Malo. The Roman tiled roofs sit well on them too, and the render, when used, is a white cement mix and yellowish in colour. The overall effect is very felicitous. Everything here is suddenly much tidier, more kempt and in better order. Smart cars line the drives of new and old houses or zoom past me on their way to Cholet. I am on the D 752 which is the only road that leads due south and which is quite a busy link with the city. I very much wish I were not on it as the early morning traffic is dense, fast and driven by hard-pushed workers with a cigarette in one hand and a mobile in the other paying scant attention to the lone walker who is forced to spend a couple of hours alertly dodging danger. There isn't much of a verge so I am for ever taking a few steps on tarmac then clambering about between roadside shrubs and trees as the traffic roars past.

Other pedestrian users of this road have not fared so well. There is a dead animal on average every fifteen metres either squashed irretrievably into the tarmac or lying on the verge and I trip up over them frequently. I try to avoid busy D roads such as this (i.e. the thick ones that are coloured yellow or brown on the map) but sometimes am forced to take them because there is no alternative. There is often not much more to do on such roads so I research this painlessly. Corpses include dogs, cats and hedgehogs (to be expected); stone martens; badgers; a wide variety of birds including an owl; salamanders; lizards (two of which are bright green and 40 cm long); many snakes and slow-worms; frogs; toads; weasels; mice and rats; on wet days a long line of squashed snails and slugs of many different species. The most common insects are hornets followed by praying mantis and cicadas (the smaller insects no doubt stick to the cars that hit them).

The road narrows and the traffic eases just south of Les Epesses where there is a sudden and dramatic change in the landscape. The little meadows on either side full of fat cattle are now littered with huge smooth boulders the size and height of cars, lying as if placed there by a giant from a forgotten age. Three cranes, like pre-historic birds, take off from among a pile of these boulders and glide effortlessly over a lake which also has a cluster of boulders emerging out of the still water. A cow standing on a boulder looks like a statue fixed on a stone base until it moves its head to watch me walking past. Wooden and stone crosses at cross roads or at the entrances to old houses are now well looked after with neatly-tended flower beds and painted gates. A small iron cross stands atop a tall Doric granite column at the entrance to a big house.

At first sight the tower of the church of St. Michel Mont Mercure looks like a natural finger of rock with a large statue on top but as I draw closer I can see that the tower is delicately perforated towards the top and that the statue is a vast greeny-blue St. Michael with his wings outstretched. It is an astonishing triumph of engineering because the statue seems so big in comparison with the slender pierced steeple to which it is fixed. The small metal base which attaches it to the stonework of the tower doesn't look strong enough to withstand the tremendous strain of a strong wind which the outstretched wings would catch like a sail at sea. The whole village with the church in the centre is built on a large outcrop of rock which is the highest point in La Vendée and the magnificent statue dominates the view for miles. I climb to the church up a steep rocky path with St. Michael towering most dramatically above me. Half-way up the tower, leaning out and pointing over a balustrade, is a group of brave people with good heads for heights; beneath them the faithful begin to pour out of the west door after Sunday morning Mass. A notice proudly proclaims that I am now on the highest point and as I move round the outside of the church I have a magnificent uninterrupted 360 degree view. I look south in the direction where I shall be walking over the next few days. The distances are overwhelming and I am reminded with a shock that there is still a very long way to go. The country looks very flat and dull right up to the horizon.

On the outskirts of Pouzauges the road passes through a wood with a steep bank on one side. Here there is a big upright slab of granite commemorating in gold letters the parish priest Abbé Gabriel Blanchard who on 25 August 1944 was able to stop reprisals being carried out against villagers who were lined up on this spot just where the land rises steeply. It is dark, eerie, very secluded and just the place to commit an atrocity away from the public view. It is hard to imagine the fear among the victims and their distraught families as Father Gabriel persuaded the tormentors to go no further and the relief and gratitude that all will have felt the following day at a Mass of thanksgiving. Although they are not mentioned, this is also a monument to the German soldiers who responded to a voice of humanity and reason. The last line of the commemoration, 'Pouzauges reconnaissant', is a dignified understatement of the whole village's gratitude to their priest.

Today is the *Journée du Patrimoine* when there is free access to all French heritage sites. At least I thought it was free until I saw my host for this evening charging each visiting adult €3 for the privilege of walking round the outside of his old Priory where I am staying the night. No-one is allowed to visit the inside of the house. There is a table on the drive just inside the gate with a couple of glossy books open at the right page and piles of postcards of the Priory at different seasons of the year. The *Patrimoine* visitors are much more important than the walker who stands shabbily to one side kicking the dust from his feet. Every now and again Monsieur asks me a question, his eyes fixed intently on the other visitors milling round the table and he pays no attention to my answers. I have just walked 33 kilometres and all I want is a hot shower and a sleep.

'You're not a real pilgrim?'

'No'.

With that I am left waiting. When he finally decides to show me to my room he introduces me to his wife who regards me with considerable loathing and extends an unwilling hand. The 'Do's and Don'ts' sheet in a plastic folder in my room says it all: 'We would ask you to walk round the gardens and the house in suitable attire. You may wear a swimming costume around the pool but wear a wrap on the way back to your room. There are three places where you may dry your costumes and your washing. They are hidden from view so please use them, and for pity's sake remember we are not in Sicily and we do not wish to see washing hanging out of the bedroom windows!!!!!!'. This is a translation of the original French and the six exclamation marks are entirely genuine.

I have a perfectly adequate room although the bed is a bit hard. Through a locked door I can hear a clock striking the hour, and three minutes later it strikes again. Many French clocks have a repeat striking mechanism like this. Despite a very heavy shower of rain just after my arrival I have managed to walk round the garden and take some photos. There are a number of fine old yew trees clipped into neat egg shapes in the English style and an area which

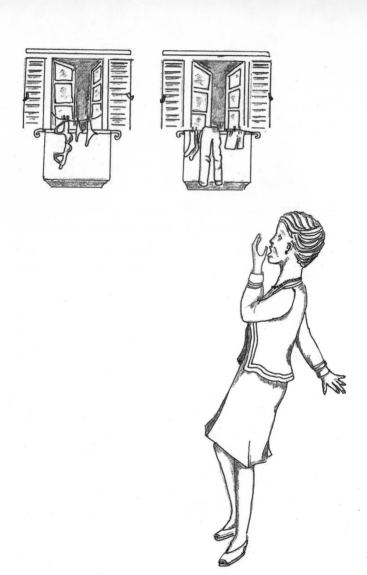

'For pity's sake remember we are not in Sicily and we do not wish to see washing hanging out of the bedroom windows!!!!!!'.

has just been replanted. There are two donkeys too and a vegetable garden in which I am greatly amused to see a fat Mr MacGregor rabbit gorging itself on the cabbages.

The most interesting bit by far is inside an old outbuilding which they use as cellarage. When they came to restore the room next door they discovered beneath the mud render a 14th century chapel window with trifolium and another smaller window next to it. There is a thick stone wall built right through the window so restoring it will be difficult and costly involving an architect. I eavesdrop on this while Madame is talking to a man I think she already knows who tells her of a fund that she could approach for the money. I comment on the hollow in the main wall just to the right of the window which I suggest might originally have been for keeping the water and wine for use during Mass but I get no reaction from the owner. She pays no attention whatsoever to me despite the fact that all three of us are standing together in the outhouse examining the window and trying to imagine this building as an ancient Priory chapel.

Monsieur, who is now trying hard (Madame having retreated inside the house), has suggested I go to the bar Le Rétro in the village that should be open on a Sunday evening and should do meals. In the same breath he says I can breakfast with him in the morning (Madame isn't mentioned), and shows me their dining room, a pleasant room with a stone floor and heavy furniture (as is so often the case) and also the *pendule* (grandfather clock) that I can hear from my room. He asks if I mind so I immediately say how agreeable it is to hear clocks again for the first time since the start of my walk, that I have clocks as well and that they never disturb me at night. But he doesn't listen, preferring to say that they have four *pendules* in the house and then waits for my adulatory response which he doesn't get because I think it is quite normal for someone who likes clocks to have so many. He has a bright Steradent smile and is still quite a good-looking man in his late seventies or early eighties. His eyes, however, are a touch disconcerting as they are the colour of stagnant water and look without seeing.

I decide to try my luck at the Rétro bar. After all, even a plate of chips with a slab of plastic pizza would be better than my soggy sandwiches, so off I go, not expecting very much. It is full of young men with their wives, girlfriends and children watching Paris S.G. play Monaco on an enormous flat screen TV. They buy their beer in 2 litre jugs then top up individual glasses as the levels go down. I am asked if I want 'Kro' (short for 'Kronenbourg) or anything else. I opt for 'Kro' because I cannot see anything else on offer. More importantly, I cannot see any sign of food, and the Madame behind the bar is as engrossed as everyone else in the football match and would not want to go and kick start her kitchen just for one measly meal.

I go back somewhat forlornly to my room and peel the cling film from my sandwiches. The worst has occurred in that the filling has become fused with the outer layer of soggy bread and bits of tuna ooze through the bread as I try to eat it. Fortunately my appetite disappears but later

Monsieur asks if I ate well at Le Rétro. When I tell him the story he offers me two wrinkled peaches the size of walnuts and three tiny cherry tomatoes from the garden which I accept and wolf down as soon as he is out of sight. Seconds later I can hear them through the interconnecting door having their supper. The clink and chink of glasses and cutlery is almost unbearable. I ask myself what I would have done if I ran a *chambre d'hôte* and one of my guests clearly had had no supper, but I fall asleep before I can get anywhere near answering the question.

Breakfast is stale toasted *baguette* but there is also some wholemeal bread which is fresh enough, an apple from the garden and a couple of home-made jams. Monsieur presides, toasts the bread then crunches on it very noisily, says what a fine region La Vendée is because unemployment is lower than average, then admits that he has had 'real' pilgrims here before. He has lived in Africa where he came across people who walked 30 kilometres to work and 30 kilometres back every day carrying tremendous weights on their heads, and all for a pittance.

Madame emerges in the middle of all this, wrapped in a dressing gown, dishevelled and silent, but has the grace to say 'bonne route' and 'mind your head' when I leave. I think she cannot handle the fact that I am a walker; a pilgrim may be just acceptable, but not a walker. Had I arrived on a polo pony then all would have been fine, but a man who walks alone through France and who is not a pilgrim cannot be trusted. Had I been able to eat with them last night, and indeed had they been just a little more welcoming, I might have let slip that there was a time when this scruffy walker had dined and spent the night *chez* the Comte de Paris, he who today would be on the throne of France. I could have dwelt for some time on the lavishly appointed apartment with its heavy mahogany door covered with lots of polished brass; the pink *décor* glowing in the electric light; the flunkies keeping at a discreet distance; dinner consisting of a couple of large birds (ducks? geese?) that came from the kitchen on platters with their heads still on so they looked very much alive albeit somewhat charred; a night spent in a sumptuously comfortable bed inside an alcove generously draped with pink silk. Had I spoken of all this Madame might have been better disposed towards me.

Hoping that she notices me from the drawing room, I leave with wet socks and a tee shirt dangling from my backpack and a pair of damp underpants on my left arm. It takes some ingenuity to do this involving threading the arm more than once through the holes in the garment, but it can be done. It must be the left arm because that will get all the early-morning sun as I move south. I know a number of people who wear their faith, or their honour, or their integrity on their sleeve. I, on the other hand, have now taken to wearing my underpants. This walk, among other things, certainly is beginning to have its absurd side.

The church at Cheffois could have been picked up and transplanted here from much further south. The stone is almost golden, the roof tiled and the tower quite squat. My road twists up a hill beyond the village and all of a sudden the house names and other markers disappear so I

82

am forced yet again to rely exclusively on my compass. It is at this moment of total concentration that a very loud noise like a siren comes from one of the factories on the outskirts of the village below me. It is so loud that it bounces off trees and walls and plays havoc with my ear drums. It is not a fire-station siren for it goes on and on without a break. I note it is exactly 10:30 am so perhaps it is a siren marking the end or the beginning of the workers' shift, but after a few more minutes I reject that idea. It has successfully taken my mind off concentrating on my bearings so I resort to asking one of the locals which is always a plan of action that is fraught with danger because no-one seems to know very much at all about where they live. I approach and ask the lady for directions in French before I notice the English number plate in the drive. The background noise is still very loud so we have to shout. She is immediately confused and cups her ears to get rid of the noise while she thinks. It appears that the noise happens regularly for there is a look of grim resignation on her face. I feel sorry for her: she's an amiable lady, probably in her late sixties, living in this pretty little cottage with three or four neighbours on either side and a recently installed pool. She and her husband found the house at the beginning of the summer, fell in love with it and completed all the paperwork before discovering the noise nuisance from the factory across the valley. I don't have the heart to question her more about it and anyway she is impatient to shut herself inside out of its full blast. I have walked 4 kilometres by the time it ends, subsiding like a siren until once again the normal countryside noises can be heard. It is now ten past eleven so we have had forty minutes of uninterrupted hell.

I think it must be my double tail caused by dangling socks that makes the cattle go berserk. For the second time a large herd comes running to the fence, but instead of trying to vault it this time in total silence each beast begins to bellow and they all follow me on their side of the fence bellowing as I walk past. A shutter swings open in the farm house up the track and a woman peers cautiously out then a man appears at the door. Although he is at least a hundred metres away I can quite clearly see the deep furrows on his brow. The bellowing gets even louder when I reach the end of the field for my road turns in such a way that the cattle have an uninterrupted view of my swinging socks and sticks for another ten minutes. Another farmer appears outside his door and stares, hands on hips.

In the middle of a crossroads I see the sort of road sign that used to be very common many years ago. Made of cement, it is the same shape as a metre-high capstan with four rectangular sides at the top, on each of which are painted in dark blue the names of villages and arrows pointing in the right direction. I am delighted to see that someone is looking after it for it stands in a small round bed full of pink geraniums and purple verbena.

Just on my right up a steep hill is a modern sign advertising Vouvant as a *cité de caractère* with a fine ancient church so I turn off the road and climb up to it. Actually, if the truth be known, I am more motivated by the prospect of a *plat du jour* at the *auberge* than the unquestionably delightful

84

Romanesque church that I decide to leave until after my hunger pangs have been attended to. As I walk up towards the centre I am astonished by the number of English voices in gardens and drifting out of windows and the numerous English number plates outside the houses. The menu at the *auberge* (maddeningly closed through change of ownership) includes 'Fish and chips every Thursday' and 'Sunday roast and dessert' all written in English. The French man in the *tabac* whose wife has made me a sandwich tells me that most of the inhabitants are English and that some very dodgy property deals have recently taken place involving handing over private cheques after the official sale has gone through. This has led to considerable ill feeling for official house prices are high enough as it is thanks to the influx of all the English people. At the *tabac* end of the bar there are piles of different English newspapers and magazines and one small pile of the local French paper. An English couple in the bar who ask for their beers in English say how disappointed they were when the 'pub' in their village a few miles away closed down. They are using this year's English OAPs' fuel allowance to pay for their daughter and family to join them for Christmas. I am glad to get away.

I always find it difficult to get moving again after a prolonged rest and today is no exception so the last 8 kilometres to Foussais-Payré are a bit painful but my welcome at the *chambre d'hôte* the best yet. Madame is quite a star: musical, sings and is organising a tour taking Mozart's *Requiem* from Nantes to Cholet via a host of other places in November; does remarkable patchwork which is on display all over the house; and is an ex-tennis star with silver cups, suitably engraved, to prove it. Monsieur is proud of his library; used to work for IBM and knows Portsmouth and the State of New York where they lived for two years. At some stage during a grand tour of the house and garden I say they have so many apples in the orchard they could make cider, but then Madame says they don't like alcohol and my heart sinks.

Madame has to go to a choir practice (back at 11 pm) so Monsieur is left in charge of serving and carving the chicken, something he has never done before. He finds this and all the timings rather difficult. I, on the other hand, find it charming. We have an excellent Kir for the *apéritif* with proper Aligoté and a bottle of Chénas with the meal. He is half Burgundian and likes his wines so my initial worries about alcohol turn out to be unfounded. The word 'alcool' in French when talking about drink in general means 'spirits', not simply 'alcohol' and they must have thought I meant something like Calvados when I mentioned making cider earlier on.

We speak a lot about books over dinner and he keeps popping out and coming back with reference books to look up and prove a point. Eventually the conversation comes round to Les Deux Sèvres through which I am walking tomorrow and he, quite understandably, can't explain why there is an 's' after Sèvres. Normally French names don't take an 's' in the plural, but, according to my host, 'Sèvre might because it is not a family name'. There is probably a simpler reason: there are two rivers, one called La Sèvre

Niortaise, the other La Sèvre Nantaise, and because they are separate entities they take an 's' in the plural. This is just the sort of conversation that demands a long time so we carry on till Madame gets back. She gently chides her husband for not having cut more bread and urges me to take more cheese.

If I thought dinner ordinary she says (despite loud and genuine protests from me), then just wait till breakfast. Indeed, Pantagruel would have approved: two warm hard-boiled eggs (she says she can't guarantee being able to produce soft-boiled); a pot of pigeon pâté; a pear *clafoutis* freshly made this morning that would have done for four; home-made apple juice and jams; a basket of bread and *croissants*. All this and a wide selection of teas that lie on the table on a large tray. It is not easy to leave such warm and genuine hospitality particularly when the heavens open and the rain shows no sign of easing, but leave I must as Niort is a long way off and I know that wet weather slows me down. Could I please be sure to e-mail them when I finally arrive at my destination.

It is quite clear on the map that my little road goes under the motorway then swings south east and goes all the way to Niort. But no. My road has been ploughed over and there is nothing in its place except a field of dead sunflowers. The compass brings me to a few kilometres from where I need to be and then nothing; no sign posts, no points of reference and even no indication on the map that there is a single-track railway on my right. Again I have to fall back on local knowledge in the form of an old lady who spots me through her kitchen window and comes to my help.

'Is this the road to Richebonne?' (an amusing place name meaning 'rich servant' that casts the only gleam of light on an otherwise damp and grey morning).

'Yes sir. Richebonne is behind those trees. *Un petit kilomètre. Enfin, un petit kilomètre élastique.*'

It is a perfect image for her to have chosen for it is like that old elastic that you pull and pull only to find that it makes no effort to go back to its original shape. Richebonne is a full four kilometres from the old lady's house and it is here that I am forced to take the Route Nationale to Niort because my little road has yet again disappeared.

It is not a nice experience because the speeding lorries create such wind and suction that my sticks are blown into my legs causing me to stumble frequently. The road is dead straight with just one or two gentle inclines that hide the view of the city until much later. On either side the land stretches away getting bluer and bluer until it reaches the horizon. There are no trees and no hills to break the view. All I can see are vast fields on either side, full of winter wheat and sorghum and not a single farm animal grazing. I go past an empty shell of a building that used to be a restaurant. The windows are all broken and there is a fading advertisement for Pernod painted on one of the gable ends. Grass grows up through the cracks of tarmac and cement where customers used to park.

There is a broad sweep of litter on the side of the road that people have thrown out of their cars. I am becoming quite accustomed to this and have so far since St. Malo gone past countless cigarette packets with the words *FUMER TUE* (smoking kills) outlined in bold; syringes (all artfully dodged in time); Macdonald's containers; whole cartons of (empty) beer and wine bottles; dolls and cuddly toys; used nappies; very bizarrely, an extraordinarily large number of pieces of wire, average length 1 – 2 metres; thousands and thousands of plastic water bottles; human excrement with tell-tale piles of tissues (quite common); full bin liners (occasionally suspended from branches); items of clothing and shoes; a small gold cross which I am happy to return to the owner if his/her description fits and if they can give the approximate location.

When Niort finally looms into view it looks rather small with just half a dozen high-rise blocks on one side and three fine steeples on the other. The tallest building is an oversized water tower quite close to the city centre which makes me think that achieving water pressure for a city of more than 125000 inhabitants in such a flat area must be an engineering nightmare. I become more and more impressed with Niort as I get closer to the centre. Many of the suburban houses stand back from the road in the midst of good gardens with mature shrubs and trees. As I walk under a bridge I am struck by the high quality of the graffiti: faces and figures with real tone and this is repeated elsewhere in the city. I never thought I would approve of graffiti but some of this is really good. I know that in Barcelona good graffiti artists are employed by the city council in an attempt to dissuade the poorer artists from leaving their mark.

Perhaps the Niort civic authorities have done the same, but with a greater degree of success.

There are some very fine 18th century façades with no ornamentation overlooking the river and, surprisingly, a number of different levels in the centre: twisting, narrow streets filled with colourful shops, bars and restaurants. Waiters stand on pavements trying to entice in passers-by to sample the fare. It is a funny feeling to be spoilt for choice for a change. Up till now I have only come across at best a *brasserie* serving a *menu* with a *plat du jour,* at worst a café with the standard two things on offer: frozen pizza or *croque monsieur.* A cheap *menu* in a *brasserie* is around €10 for three courses which at first sight seems good value but the fast food manufacturers appear to have cornered the entire market and nothing is home-made. The first course is invariably a cold buffet consisting of a number of tinned salads (grated carrot; grated celeriac; pasta with peas, diced ham and mayonnaise etc.), two or three varieties of low quality *pâtés*, and gherkins preserved in a fierce vinegar. The fast food manufacturers even appear to supply the refrigerated trolley holding the different dishes for they turn out to be all the same from St. Malo down to the Gers: stainless steel cabinets with a clear plastic roof complete with neon light that rises and switches on at the touch of a button. The main course is chicken thigh, or steak, or pork delivered with a sauce and served with tinned *haricots verts* beans or frozen chips. Pudding is a slice of pastry, *crème caramel* or *îles flottantes* (which in fact would sink if served in a larger quantity of *crème anglaise*). The cook in such establishments does no more than wield an opener and turn on the heat where required. It is certainly cheering to see these places quite full at lunchtime but the standard of food served is very low. Worse still are the snacks in cafés which I have to resort to a number of times.

La cuisine française is a sacred cow which one criticises at one's peril, but on the whole so far I have eaten badly. Let it be said from the start that there is no place like France for excellent food at low prices. One can eat more deliciously in France at between €18 – €25 than anywhere else, and beyond that price range one can enter culinary Heaven. I am certainly not griping about that, but it must be remembered that I have been on the whole miles away from main roads so the places I have stumbled across are in the middle of the country and always modest. Here in Niort, however, there are cheap restaurants with sight lines going through to the kitchens in which there are real cooks cooking real food and there are delicious food smells everywhere.

One street, known locally as 'Les Serpents' has a novel form of bollard in the shape of long bronze serpents snaking along the kerb on each side to stop cars parking. I chance upon an ancient door with well-worn stone surrounds and a family crest that has been obliterated over the centuries. In the town centre is an imposing glass and steel structure, essentially 19th century in style, which houses the market and as I move round it I see the different views reflected in the glass: the crenellated turrets of the medieval castle on one side, the twin steeples of a church on the other. The most imposing building in town is the early 19th century *Mairie*, perched at the top of a hill with its proud steeply-pitched slate roof pierced with *mansarde* windows, capped by a bell tower, the front elevation faced with stone.

My hotel room looks over the south elevation of a church with a fine slate steeple and a clock (not working) just beneath it. In between there is a garden with a long high wall of rabbit hutches piled one on top of the other and I see a man emerging from the house with a box of vegetable peelings that he gives them to eat. A child on a tricycle pokes a stick into a hutch and squeals with delight when the rabbit leaps out of range.

In the evening I sit at a bar with a cool drink and overhear a conversation between a man in sinister dark glasses, a smart suit over a black shirt and white tie, and the barman who shifts uneasily from one foot to the other. The man is a debt collector and outlines a scheme whereby the bar could remain open provided an agreed amount is paid off before a certain date. Towards the end of the conversation he says 'We are only here to help. We are not the *gendarmes*'. After the grimly-dressed man has shaken hands and taken his leave the barman angrily pushes a few buttons on his 'phone, speaks some obscenities into the receiver to a friend and looks very miserable indeed. He goes and stands on the pavement outside, lights a cigarette and angrily fills his lungs with smoke, muttering darkly to himself.

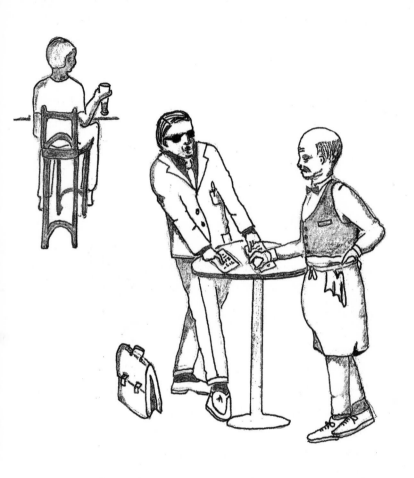

In the evening I sit at a bar and overhear a
conversation between a man in sinister dark
glasses and the barman.

5

La Sèvre Niortaise – La Charente

According to the map my road out of Niort goes under the railway line then on to Chizé. In reality, however, not so. The very obvious tunnel on the map simply isn't there. I can certainly see the road on the other side of the railway but no legitimate means of getting on to it so in the end, I have to enter someone's garden, insert myself through a gap in his fence, cross the line and do the same thing in reverse on the other side. I was not expecting these maps to contain serious errors but IGN maps (Institut Géographique National) cannot be relied on totally and often the walker has to be prepared to re-think his itinerary on the spot. There have already been a number of occasions when my road, which should have gone on for miles according to the map, simply petered out and became a field.

The flat landscape persists beyond Niort and there is nowhere private and few trees to break the view. All the farms and houses are at least a kilometre away from the road down a track with few signs on the road saying what lies at the end of the track. It cannot be much fun being a trainee postman round here. It's not much fun being a walker either as the horizon seems to get no closer and the distances between villages and settlements seem endless. I hardly pass a car or see another human being for what seems like hours.

The road crosses a series of dry ditches each of which is awarded its own name on a sign as if it were a proper river. Small road bridges crossing ditches and streams are of a standard design seen all over France: a low stone wall on each side of the road with the end stones picked out in white paint. It is an odd fact that there are no interesting bridges of local design here, unlike in Britain where minor bridges tend to vary in construction. I don't count here of course the many Roman bridges that on the whole are well preserved.

The village bar/restaurant at Chizé advertises a choice of *plat du jour*: either pig's cheeks or *filet mignon* with tinned boiled potatoes or flageolet beans. We are eleven solo diners sitting at two long tables with litre flagons of chilled red wine and water down the middle. The waitress, a buxom young thing with a basso voice, asks each of us what we want, the cheeks or the steak. Half a dozen of us ask for the steak but when it arrives it is quite clearly cheeks, not steak. No-one says anything but we all set to and begin to eat. The same thing happens at the other table in that most are given things they haven't ordered. It happens again with pudding: I ask for *crème caramel* and get a soggy tart, and so on up and down the table. I try to catch a neighbour's eye but they are all intent on eating, not seeming to care that they are eating the wrong dish. If this were a comedy skit on TV the studio audience would die laughing looking at a group of grown men and women asking for one thing in a restaurant then accepting something entirely different and eating it in total and approving silence.

Whenever I lean back my one-size-fits-all-man-made-fibre-tee-shirt sticks to the back of my chair and when I pull it away it makes a noise like Velcro. I notice that all the chairs have layers of black grime on them where sticky fingers have touched them over the years. Above the bar is an invitation to a *Thé Dansant* later today and on the wall a poster entitled 'Sauvons les Cafés Français: Signez la Pétition'. I suspect this bar's chances of survival are almost zero and I am seriously tempted to wait until 6:30 this evening to see what precisely they mean by a *Thé Dansant* and how they go about organising it.

By the side of the road near Aulnay is a small monument with a white marble plaque commemorating two resistance fighters who were shot on this spot on 25 August 1944, the same date that Father Gabriel Blanchard was able to stop reprisals at Pouzauges. At the base of the monument is an enamel plaque reproducing General de Gaulle's exhortation dated June 1940 to all French men and women to resist the enemy with all the means at their disposal.

A TOUS LES FRANÇAIS

La France a perdu une bataille!

Mais la France n'a pas perdu la guerre !

Des gouvernants de rencontre ont pu capituler, cédant à la panique, oubliant l'honneur, livrant le pays à la servitude.

Cependant, rien n'est perdu !

Rien n'est perdu, parce que cette guerre est une guerre mondiale. Dans l'univers libre, des forces immenses n'ont pas encore donné. Un jour, ces forces écraseront l'ennemi. Il faut que la France, ce jour-là, soit présente à la victoire. Alors, elle retrouvera sa liberté et sa grandeur. Tel est mon but, mon seul but !

Voilà pourquoi je convie tous les Français, où qu'ils se trouvent, à s'unir à moi dans l'action, dans le sacrifice et dans l'espérance.

Notre patrie est en péril de mort.

Luttons tous pour la sauver !

VIVE LA FRANCE ! [1]

---

[1] To all French men and women: France has lost a battle! But France has not lost the war! Spurious leaders have seen fit to capitulate, yielding to panic, ignoring honour, delivering the country up to servitude. However, nothing is lost! Nothing is lost, because this war is a world war. The strongest forces have yet to be unleashed in the free world. One day, these forces will crush the enemy. On that day France must be present at the victory. Then she will recover her liberty and her greatness. That is my aim, my only aim! That is why I invite all French people, wherever they may be, to join with me in active resistance, sacrifice and hope. Our fatherland is in deadly peril. Let us all fight to save it! Long live France!

This will have been widely distributed and read by all who were active in the Resistance movement and certainly these two commemorated here will have been familiar with it. It is worth pausing for a moment to think of what the full consequences may have been to this country if the Allies had suffered defeat.

The tiny Romanesque church at Salle lès Aulnay with its deeply carved entrance is as striking in its simplicity as the grander church at Aulnay which is a real gem and well worth a long journey to visit. Originally it stood by itself well outside the village but now ugly little houses have encroached on either side and a garish yellow neon sign facing the magnificent West Door advertises the pizza parlour behind. The church can easily withstand all this, however, and is very, very special. As I walk round a steady stream of tourists appear in buses and private cars and chatter noisily to each other. With the flat landscape all around, the tower can be seen from quite far away looking very dramatic against an angry sky.

In between heavy showers I see vast flocks of birds enjoying the strong wind and the damp, wheeling and swirling before me then suddenly flying to the other side of my field of vision and repeating the same fluttering movements, the wind blowing and spots of rain splattering all the while. All this energy and life and then, there in the ditch twitching helplessly after hitting a vehicle last night lies a tawny owl, still beautiful but already condemned and with fear of the unknown in its shiny black eyes. I stand and look at it for some time trying to summon up the courage to despatch it out of its misery but am unable to. I decide, probably wrongly, that it would prefer to be left to die in peace.

Just as I resume my walk a lorry travelling too fast comes round the bend and the driver, taking exception to the fact that, with a deep ditch on my left, I have to occupy a few centimetres of the tarmac, swerves straight at me giving a full blast of his siren and forces me into the ditch. I am five or six metres away from the owl and only too aware of the irony of what has just happened. This is the only time I have to put up with such a thing for on the whole drivers signal and pull over giving me plenty of room. The worst etiquette so far has been displayed by cyclists who, to a man (it is a very male-dominated sport), stick doggedly to their course and refuse even a slight swerve. I learned very early on to get well out of their way.

Matha is a charming little place, not very beautiful, but the people have a smile. When the chemist learns where I am staying he says it is just the right sort of place for 'une personne de votre qualité' (someone of your distinction), and we both burst out laughing. There is bunting all over town with a preponderance of Union Jack flags and stickers in shop windows saying Bienvenue/Welcome against a red, white and blue background. I pause to admire a display for the beginning of the school year in a grocer's shop window entitled 'Vive la Rentrée' with a selection of old school photographs and an outdated English grammar book opened at the page for telling the time: 'What o'clock is it? Your watch is fast, mine is slow'. The photograph from the 1950s shows poorly fed and clothed children standing in stark contrast to this year's class gaily decked out in the latest Designer styles. The standard of living today bears no resemblance to that of merely fifty years ago. The *château* stands on the outskirts of the village and is the smallest *château* I have ever seen, occupying about as much ground as a suburban villa. But it has a fine oak door at the top of a stone stair and looks out over a stream full of watercress spanned by an ancient bridge.

I spend the night at L'Olivier, a large town house in Matha, converted into a *chambre d'hôte* and well regarded in the village, belonging to Phil and Jane, both English. They tell me that a month ago there was quite a strong earthquake at night here and in nearby Cognac, over 4 on the Richter scale. 'Things jingled and jangled for it seemed like an hour' but apparently it only lasted for a minute or two. It did nothing for Jane's confidence. She has only been here since May, misses her parents dreadfully and finds communicating in French very difficult. Phil has been here for some years and so is more settled, works with a builder and does odd jobs locally and, although far from fluent, can make himself understood. Their life-line is BBC Digital (card available for £20 from E-bay) and an extremely well-stocked video and DVD library. They are both lonely with a dearth of friends their own age and yet they are determined to remain here even when they retire. They have bought the house next door as their old-age pension complete with its elderly female occupant and four cats and they will get full ownership as soon as she dies. They are both obviously very shrewd and Phil puts me to shame as we watch a quiz programme over our drinks because he knows the answer to all the questions. I suggest he should go in for it because he could win a lot of money but he tells me he is too camera-shy.

Over a delicious dinner cooked by Jane they tell some hilarious stories about past guests sleeping on the sofas and easy chairs downstairs because they couldn't stand their partners. On one occasion some time ago when Phil was running the *chambre d'hôte* by himself, he came down in the morning and saw 'a woman in pants and see-through top *but* about fifty eight' fully stretched out on a sofa, scared of going back to the bedroom. I thought it best not to ask for more details.

He confesses to having a soft spot for chickens which is a reaction against his father who ran a chicken battery farm. Phil started with a couple of cockerels in the back garden here, recommended by a man in the village as a good way of stopping the next-door cats from fouling his grass. But the plan misfired and cockerels and cats quickly began getting on well together. So he put some hens with them which made the cockerels fight so badly that one of them died. 'We didn't have the heart to put it in a *pot au foo*', he says wistfully.

In the morning I discover that one of the big advantages of staying in an English B&B is that a full English breakfast is considered the norm: first cereals, then bacon and home-laid eggs, and then, to finish off, a normal French breakfast of fresh *baguette* and *croissant*. That's more like it. Jane is the third person to ask me to be sure to let them know when I arrive safely. It is curiously comforting to have complete strangers looking out for me. I am enjoying the experience of solitude but I know that I am enjoying it only because it is going to be short-lived. I have to admit that having company last night and this morning has been a very welcome break. True solitude, with an ever-present spectre of loneliness, I would find very difficult to live with.

Not far from Matha is the small village of Thors which has a delightful, really simple Romanesque church with a pierced belfry but on its south side the commune has erected a modern steel and glass bus shelter and tied it into the ancient fabric of the church. This is vandalism of the worst sort. Beyond the offending bus shelter, right up against the church wall, are the recycling bins no doubt positioned there by the same people that supported the bus shelter. On the outskirts of the village fixed to a handsome stone gatepost that once led to a substantial property is an old metal sign forbidding all begging in the village. It strikes me as very odd that in an earlier age Christian charity was frowned upon by the inhabitants of this tiny village which consists of no more than a handful of houses and a church. I wonder whether the priest himself obeyed the ruling.

Further on in the direction of Jarnac is a charming and most unusual village called quite simply Les Vignes. Here there are high stone walls broken occasionally by heavy wooden doors under arches through which can be seen the dwelling house straight ahead and the wine *chais* on either side. There are vines growing whenever there is a gap in the wall. Street names are pretty basic: rue des Vignes; rue de l'Alambic. An old couple shout at their barking dog to be quiet as I pass by while younger people in the outhouses busy themselves with the first of the grape harvest that arrives in leak-proof trailers. The sweet smell of the new wine fermenting permeates everything and in the fields just outside the village are heaps of crushed grapeskins of a rich ochre colour. One field contains a wild meadow mix of late flowering plants, rich reds and mauves, oranges and whites that look spectacular in the wan sunshine showing weakly through the thin cloud.

The next village, Bréville, is disappointing in comparison. Instead of vines here there are sawmills and woodworkers whose wooden statues are dotted all over the village. In the centre three sizeable polished beams carved to represent father, mother and child hold up a half wine barrel that has been converted into a clock. Down by the river a two-metre tall scantily clad nymph covered in peeling varnish gazes out over the water, and in front of the *Mairie*, instead of bollards, there are wooden posts carved to represent the Gallic cock, grape clusters and lusty women.

As I enter Jarnac the heady smell of the new wine fermenting hangs over this part of town. The buildings have solid stone façades and hide a good deal of wealth behind them. I pass the rue Delamain and approach a huge building in the main square with COURVOISIER written in large stand-up letters on the roof. The cafés and restaurants are doing a brisk trade with mainly English tourists and little pleasure boats bob on the river Charente to my right.

Beyond the bridge the river divides with one water course flowing beneath the flour mill. It is a busy town with plenty of heavy lorries passing through on their way to Cognac and beyond.

This is the place where François Mitterrand was born and where he chose to be buried. In a small square with a garden where children play noisily is an upright stone slab with *François Mitterrand 1916-1996 Président de la République* written on the front and a life-size sculpture of his head on top of it. He is very fondly remembered round here and is a ready topic of conversation in shops and bars: those that are old enough speak of him almost with devotion.

My *chambre d'hôte* this evening is up the hill on one of the main roads entering the town from the east. The house is a spectacular 19th century mansion standing back from the road in a garden of mature trees. To one side is a very beautiful serpentine swimming pool dating from the 1950s with a lovely stone statue on one of the curves standing in a stone shell that drips water into the pool when the pool is up and running. The magic of this place is somewhat diminished by the modern bright green fence that has been erected recently to comply with last year's law to protect young children from falling into pools and meeting with an untimely death. The front door is on the first floor reached by a stone horseshoe-shaped stairway with brick balustrades on either side. Inside there are polished wooden and tiled floors, heavy Napoleon (19th century) furniture and light fittings, ormolu clocks, oil paintings and family portraits.

The doors all have original handles and finger plates. Two rooms downstairs on either side of the front door each contain a large table that is already laid for tomorrow's breakfast. There seem to be a lot of people staying.

I have a sudden Proustian memory and am transported back some 50 years to a similar house which I visited with my sister in the foothills of the Pyrenees. I was eleven, she twelve and a half, when we went by ourselves all the way from Waterloo to the Gare du Nord, crossed Paris to Austerlitz, and took the overnight train south to Prat Bonrepaux, a tiny village close to St. Girons. It would be unimaginable for children of such an age to undertake such a journey by themselves nowadays. M. et Mme de Pieux were the very aristocratic parents of Michel who was a young man in his twenties whom my parents had helped at every stage of his stay in England in the mid fifties, and now his parents wanted to repay the favour. Madame met us at Prat station where we were the only ones to alight from the train. They lived in a spacious 19th century town house which seemed particularly grand to us, although there was no swimming pool, just a long, rather dull garden with flower beds picked out with concrete edgings. There were highly polished tiled and wooden floors in every room and we were told on arrival that on no account could we wear shoes inside. Madame supplied us each with a pair of over-sized slippers with felt soles and showed us how to advance by sliding over the polished surface of the floor. I soon started to use the long entrance hall as a practice ski slope much to the annoyance of our hostess. We both took an instant disliking to her and mimicked her wobbly bottom as she waddled from room to room. I was amused to discover recently (2006) a recommendation on a bottle of French liquid floor tile polish to give the final buff with a 'polishing slipper'.

Our room had one double bed with a bolster pillow and a push-button light switch (called a *poire électrique*, or 'electric pear') that hung from the ceiling above the bed head. In the bathroom was a bidet which I mistakenly used as a lavatory. We both panicked at the time but somehow managed to clean it up before Madame noticed what had happened.

She had arranged for a couple of local children to be our companions during the daytime. They taught us how to whack lizards and collect their twitching tails (a detail I find difficult to live with nowadays), and of course we learned a lot of French in the midst of which were a number of dreadful swear words which we didn't recognise as such but unwittingly let slip in the evenings. Madame was so horrified when I said something very vulgar, indeed unprintable, that she resolved there and then to telephone our parents and ask for guidance about how to deal with it. Telephoning abroad was very difficult in the mid fifties but eventually the call came through and we were both told to be particularly careful not to offend the humourless and highly sensitive lady who was looking after us.

My host in Jarnac, living in a similar house, is a warmer and more endearing person:

'I am delighted to welcome an Englishman into my home, and particularly one who speaks such remarkable French'. When I protest, embarrassed by what he has just said, he continues: 'I always say what I know to be true, not what I feel I should say'.

He is an intellectual with a gentle, impeccably courteous manner and has just published the second edition of a French-English dictionary which he shows me with considerable and justified pride. His life story begins to unfold. He was orphaned at birth and so had no family money. First he taught Philosophy at the University of Rennes and noted then how well prepared the boys from the Ecole St. Vincent always were. After a while he had saved up enough money to buy a bike and he would go regularly to St. Malo to do some sea bathing. The round trip took him some seven hours from start to finish. He then moved on to be a school inspector and suggested collaborating on a book with a teacher of six-year-olds. One year later it was published and sold a million copies. He hasn't looked back. He then had a successful career in diplomacy working in the Ivory Coast, Ethiopia and Colombia. He once motored from west to east across the continent of Africa and tells me with a twinkle in his eye that it was much more difficult than walking because of the dreadful state of the roads. Now that his dictionary is finished he is at a bit of a loose end and he can't wait to get started on another project.

'I miss it, you know'.

When I go down into the town at about 6 pm I see a dozen or so people at tables outside a *brasserie* still finishing their lunch. All around them the waiter has stacked tables and chairs and yet they still call for more coffee and brandy. In the Café de l'Union in the old centre of Jarnac a middle-aged English couple are playing non-stop snooker and feed coins into the slot at the start of every game. They are closely scrutinised by French onlookers, one of whom gives the Englishwoman advice when she has a tricky shot to play. There are guffaws of laughter when the Englishman, oblivious to French gender use, says to her 'Tu as perdu, mon chéri'. He thinks they are laughing because she has lost yet again to the superior player and joins in himself with the laughter but when the bar owner kinks his wrist and says 'Oooh, mon chéri, eh?' the laughter swells to fever pitch. They now take on a couple of local lads (with the Englishman paying) who beat them thoroughly. The bar owner has a soft spot for the Englishwoman who smiles at him every time she misses a shot, and he now gives her a game while the others drink a round of beers. It is good to see English people taking an active part in the community, trying to speak the language, and making friends with local people. I have seen precious little of this since setting out.

There is a large flat screen TV at the end of the bar which is tuned into Canal Plus. To my astonishment, the next programme, starting at 7:45 pm, is announced by a woman who is entirely naked down to the waist. No-one else bats an eyelid as they are much more interested in the progress of the snooker. I have since learned that such announcements are made quite frequently on this channel.

At the table next to mine a man sprinkles salt on his *baguette* and chips, the first chip butty I have come across in France.

6

La Charente – La Dronne

I take the GR4 (Grande Randonnée) footpath that goes due east out of Jarnac and eventually crosses my road to the south. First I have to go past the vast Courvoisier building which must be full of vats because once more the air is heavy with the heady smell of fermenting grapes. A noisy cooling unit at pavement level is keeping the temperature constant. On the outskirts of town I pass by a number of substantial dwellings which are all called *châteaux* and have standing next to them great stainless steel cylinders full of this year's vintage. On the road there are occasional spillages that have splashed over the sides of the bins brought by tractors to the places where the fruit is crushed. The great gates are all open and on either side of the yard bins are emptied into pits just inside the *chai* door where the crushing takes place. Shadowy figures within control the machinery and wave on the tractors. Everyone is far too busy to return my greeting.

The GR now becomes a proper track following the north bank of the river Charente that flows idly by. I go past two or three cars parked by the water's edge with their boots propped open revealing a broad selection of fishing rods and other fishing paraphernalia, and of course the all-important cool box. A woman drinking coffee from a flask says 'Bonjour' while the two men with her remain stonily silent, their eyes fixed on the serried ranks of rods each with a line going into the water.

My arrival at Bassac is heralded by a loud hand-rung carillon which is a rare sound in rural France. The magnificent Abbey church, part Romanesque, part Gothic, rises majestically Heavenwards and for a moment I am tempted to respond to the peal of the bells and attend Sunday Mass. There is a fine 18th century wing on the south side which must be the accommodation. The village itself is all of stone with neat, well-maintained houses and there are cars driving in from the country with people who are coming to attend Mass. The *boulangerie* is doing a brisk trade.

A smart, well-dressed lady in her fifties gets out of her car on her way into church, runs up the street and asks me where I am going and where I am from. I say I am doing my own 'Compostelle' or pilgrimage but only to St. Puy in the Gers, not all the way to Santiago. She is overwhelmed to learn that I am from Winchester and tells me of the extraordinary religious experience she had during her recent visit to the Cathedral. She was down in the crypt by the well directly beneath the high altar and suddenly felt her legs go from her and a great rush of spiritual energy. She had a similar experience later at Stonehenge.

'You must understand that both experiences fundamentally changed my life'.

She is fascinated by my walk and would love to make a pilgrimage of her own one day and experience true solitude. How am I handling it? She tries both my walking poles and eyes my backpack longingly, saying how she wishes she could compress all her belongings into a mere 7½ kilos.

'What a good idea your walk is' she says.

I admire the genuineness of her feeling and encourage her to make her own pilgrimage because she is so ideally suited to it.

'And you are from Winchester...I am so happy to have met you'. Her parting comment as she heads towards the Abbey is 'I will pray for you'.

I arrive at Châteauneuf sur Charente as the clocks strike 11:45 and think I might just have time to make it to an Intermarché supermarket directed to my left down a road on the outskirts of town next to the station. It is further than I expect so I arrive with just five minutes to go before it closes, but already the staff are pouring out and the manager on the inside of the door with a bunch of keys in his hand points to the opening hours that are crudely stuck with tape onto the glass and wags his finger. Because it is Sunday the *Buffet de la Gare* is also firmly shut as is another small bar opposite. I walk as fast as I can into the town centre in the hope of catching a shop open but all the shutters in the immediate vicinity are already down with one exception, an expensive-looking wine shop presided over by an assistant wearing a tie. I stuff an over-priced half-bottle of chilled Muscadet into my bag and rush off in search of food but there is nothing else open apart from a *boulangerie* with, so it appears, empty shelves. Next to it is a bar in the process of closing with a new notice on the door saying 'Closed until further notice on account of bereavement' first in English, then in French. The little bar opposite, however, is full of life, just the sort of place that would rustle me up a quick sandwich, but the man behind the bar tells me they don't do any food on a Sunday and that I should try the Englishman's bar across the street. He then corrects himself, says I can't go there because the Englishman's wife has just died, so why don't I go to the *boulangerie* and ask the *boulangère*. I cross the street for the third time and thankfully the door is still unlocked. There is a stray *baguette* under the counter but Madame tells me firmly that she does not make sandwiches. I ask if she has any chocolate and as she shakes her head I suggest she might give me some of the thin strips of chocolate that are used for making *pain au chocolat*. She disappears into the bakery at the back of the shop then returns and pops something begrudgingly into my paper bag. There is a solitary chocolate éclair behind a glass screen so I snap that up too.

The *Mairie* is on an island in the middle of the high street with an impressive flight of stone stairs leading to a portico held up by heavy Corinthian pillars. It is the only shade that I can find so I position myself carefully where the pigeons have not been, leaning against a pillar, gazing down at the chemist and his wife changing their shop window display during the lunch break. I now discover to my dismay that the *boulangère* put only three strips of chocolate the size of matchsticks into the bag. I thank God for the Muscadet and convince myself that, *faute de mieux,* it is an excellent wine to accompany a chocolate éclair, then nod off for a good half an hour. At three o'clock I am outside the *tabac* hoping that it will open soon so that I can buy some chocolate bars. The *tabagiste* and his wife are there tidying up and stacking cartons but they wave me away when I knock gently on the door. I try to explain the problem through the glass but immediately give up because it is quite clear they aren't going to budge an inch.

Much later in the afternoon I arrive chez Michel and Liliane Chaigneau, a couple in their 80s who do *chambre d'hôte* just south of Châteauneuf sur Charente. There is much jollity when I arrive about why I am walking such a long way and haven't I heard of the train. Liliane has offered to make me dinner tonight and I am intrigued to know what it will be like. She has already asked if there is anything I cannot eat which I take as a very good sign. My quarters are a tiny house at the bottom of the garden with one double and two single beds, a mezzanine and bathroom. Michel shows me the greenhouses and sheds in the garden filled with tiny geranium cuttings for next year and explains that Liliane is proud of the entrance to her house for there are flowers everywhere. They cascade down the façade and overspill little beds in the gravel.

It is very quiet here with just the occasional car passing along the road in front of the house. Whenever friends pass they give a toot on the horn and my hosts know who it is by simply looking at the clock: 5 pm, that must be Sylvie on her way to pick up the children; 5:15 Monique's a little late today. I sit outside my quarters looking up at the wide, wild sky filling with storm clouds and listening with some dread to an occasional clap of distant thunder.

Michel has begun to call me 'tu'. 'I am eighty, so you could be my son', he says, although Liliane sticks to the 'vous' form. He suggests going for a ride in his car which I eagerly accept. To get to the garage we have to pass through his workshop, now spotlessly clean and very tidy, where he worked as a blacksmith all his life. He and two others were responsible for shoeing about 120 horses so they had their work cut out making the shoes here then going to all the local farms and houses to fit them on the horses. When he retired at 62 he was taken on by the local newspaper as photographer for all the sports fixtures in the district and he proudly shows me his archives of all the negatives, each one labelled and filed away in the shallow drawers of a handsome steel cabinet which he himself made.

At first I find it very difficult to adjust to the speed of the car even though Michel doesn't drive fast at all. After all, this is the first time I have travelled faster than at a walking pace for many days. We drive back along the road I followed this morning covering the distance in a matter of minutes. He shows me a *gabarre*, a flat-bottomed river boat that used to transport heavy goods up and down the Charente and which originally was pulled by women. He points out six-foot high concrete pillars with an electricity meter box fixed to the top that serve the new houses built in the flood plain. A bit further on by the side of the road are two intricately carved stone pillars that stand at the entrance to a vineyard that goes with the substantial house opposite. This is where Mitterrand's brother still lives and where the President used to come on holiday.

Then we go to the 11th century St. Surin church which is abandoned but still very lovely. Under a stone arch I glimpse the old presbytery and note that the church wall doubles up as the garden wall and has plants climbing up it. The bell that used to hang in the pierced belfry is now hanging and regularly rung at the main parish church in Châteauneuf. On one inside wall, just showing through the black damp, is an ancient rust-coloured painting of a cross some two feet high. There is a makeshift altar covered with statuettes, candles, small pictures of saints and a postcard of a pilgrim with this charter. It urges the pilgrim to stick to his path in both senses of the term and contains some straightforward advice as to how we should all tackle life's pilgrimage.

Va, pèlerin,
poursuis ta quête ;
va sur ton chemin,
que rien ne t'arrête !
Prends ta part de soleil,

et part de poussière,
le cœur en éveil,
oublie l'éphémère !
Tout est néant ;
rien n'est vrai que l'amour.
N'attache pas ton cœur
à ce qui se passe.
Ne dis pas : j'ai réussi,
je suis payé de ma peine.
Ne te repose pas dans tes œuvres
elles vont te juger.
Garde en ton cœur la parole.
Voilà ton trésor.[1]

Michel proudly takes me to see all these things and shows me the best angles for photography: a view of St. Surin through an archway; a stretch of river catching the late afternoon sun; a bridge mirrored in a mill pond with a fine *château* beyond. He stops the car in the middle of a road junction in Châteauneuf to show me a medieval doorway up a lane. Another car approaches driven by a very elegant old lady in gloves who knows him well. Wonderful banter ensues. She says 'You can't park there'. He replies 'But you're

[1]   Go pilgrim, pursue your quest; go on your way and may nothing stop you! Withstand sun and dust; with a strong heart ignore all that is ephemeral! Everything is vanity; nothing is true apart from love. Do not be tempted by what is transient! Don't say: I have succeeded, my hardships have paid my debts. Don't rest on your laurels for they will pass judgement on you. Keep the Word within your heart. That is your reward.

on a yellow line', then in the car he says 'It's the hospital mocking the infirmary', a charming version of the English pot calling the kettle black. He shows me the 'hospital' at Châteauneuf which is not a hospital in the strict sense of the word but a home for the mentally handicapped. Two or three of the patients recognise him through the window and run outside to shake his hand.

I am introduced to a friend as 'a German, no, an Englishman. Oh well, what does it matter?' and this becomes the joke of the evening. Over dinner when his *gendarme* son rings from Paris, Michel says 'We've got a German staying who speaks fluent English and French'. As the wine begins to take effect he says to his second son, also ringing just for a chat, 'We've got some German here who's straight out of a pantomime, I can tell you'. But they are less flippant when they talk about their experiences with the real Germans during the war. Michel was twenty and a prisoner in Germany, Liliane fifteen and they wrote to each other throughout. The local Resistance was very strong under the inspiring leadership of Claude Bonnier, known in code as Hypotenuse, and there is a handsome memorial to him by the side of the field code-named Albatros on the banks of the river Charente where the R.A.F. dropped supplies in an operation called Water Pistol. Bonnier was later betrayed but took cyanide in case he cracked under torture for he was aware that he knew too much. The Germans were hated locally but Michel and Liliane have both made a big effort since the war to bury their prejudices. Liliane worked in the Tourist Office in Jarnac for many years where she did what

119

she could to establish good relationships with Germany but she still finds it difficult to accommodate older Germans 'with grey hair' who may have played a part in the war. One such person came to stay recently in their *chambre d'hôte* and the first thing he said to them on arrival was that he had not been in occupied France and had never used a gun against a French citizen. It made them feel better but they still found it hard.

In 1995 they organised a lorry load of aid to Rumania and followed it in a camper van borrowed from a friend to make sure that it got through to the required destination. At the frontier the guard demanded a huge bribe to let the lorry through and would not respond to their pleas. For a time they thought they would have to turn back because the sum demanded was considerable but a Polish lorry driver in the queue who had been across this frontier a few times before told them to be firm, to wait for the relief guard and then try again. The relief guard let them through.

When Mitterrand was President, Michel wrote asking him if he would be good enough to welcome a fellow *Charentais* to the Elysée Palace. Mitterrand replied in the affirmative. Could they turn up at the President's private entrance? They were particularly chuffed by this as the President's entrance is normally just that and no-one else uses it. As they waited to gain admission a helicopter flew overhead and one of the security men told them it was the President coming back from a foreign visit. They waited and then walked into the Elysée together reminiscing about their childhood, swapping stories about mutual acquaintances.

During the photo session Michel found himself suggesting to the photographer where it would be best to place the President. Mitterrand went and stood where Michel told him to.

'It was quite a *coup* you know' he says pouring out the Raisignac (a sort of Pineau but less strong and slightly sparkling).

Over dinner he uses his own Opinel knife with a wooden handle blackened by time and a blade as sharp as a razor. Liliane scolds him about the poor quality of the wine he has brought to the table so, like a naughty schoolboy, he disappears in search of another bottle. Before I retire to bed she hands me the bill which comes to €38 for dinner, bed and breakfast. Michel takes the bill, checks it and says to me in a whisper when she is out of earshot:

'That's reasonable, don't you think?'

The first two kilometres of today's walk follow the ancient Saintes - Rome route according to a sign conveniently placed at the side of the road. Then I get back on to the D10 which will eventually take me further than today's lodging (a *château* 6 km south of Blanzac). Soon the land begins to rise and continues to do so all day. Now the landscape changes to wide valleys with substantial stone-built houses sitting snugly in the folds of the hills, each with its arched gate firmly shut as a security measure while the distillation process gets underway. Up and down the road go tractors pulling modern leak-proof bins full of grapes that have just been harvested. In between the tractors can be heard the loud hum of the harvesters, very tall machines painted a striking bright blue that sit astride the rows of vines and advance at 15 - 20 kilometres per hour stripping the vines of their fruit. All the producers advertise their own Cognac and Pineau des Charentes by the side of the road. I would love to go and have a *dégustation* but decide against it since I would have no chance of making a purchase. I don't want to weigh down my backpack unnecessarily at this stage.

There is another stunningly beautiful, very small and simple Romanesque church at Etriac with a well-tended *potager* (vegetable garden) starting at the base of the east wall then plunging steeply down the hill. A small vine is trained up the wall of the church. Two women with hoes work up and down the rows and I can quite clearly hear what they are saying as their voices bounce off the church wall in my direction: their menfolk are out in the vineyards and there will be vegetable soup at lunch, *potage* straight out of the *potager*.

The *Mairie* here is attached to the school, the windows of which are wide open with satchels resting on the sills and complete silence coming from the classroom. It is probably a dreaded Monday morning test that is holding everybody's attention. The road dips then climbs again, each time a little higher until there are fewer vines and a wider acreage of cereals. These vines still have the fruit on them and there are no signs of harvesters so up here the weather must generally be cooler. When the sun hides behind a cloud the temperature falls dramatically and whenever the wind gets up large drops from last night's rain fall from the trees.

The road is very quiet and if a car or tractor passes, the driver stares hard at me as if they have never seen such a sight before. A man kitted out for walking is a most unusual sight in rural France and I can honestly say that I have not come across any other walkers since I set out. I think it is all to do with the fact that walking in France along a route other than a *Grande Randonnée* is considered at best eccentric, at worst undesirable. Walking randomly along country lanes after a good lunch is an activity in which the French do not indulge. The three miler on a Sunday afternoon doesn't exist, and since they don't exercise their dogs you come across nobody walking for the sheer pleasure of it. If you wish to walk in France you become a *randonneur* and choose your *GR,* and your *GR* club accordingly. It is the same story with cycling. In this country one doesn't go for a gentle spin on one's bike and I suspect that the bicycle clip is virtually unheard of. Here you need a racer, the full lycra kit with padded bottom, goggles and helmet to make you look like a competitor in the *Tour de France.* The sit-up-and-beg bike dear to the English academic hardly exists here, and if you happen to see a second-hand bike in a *vide grenier* (car boot sale) it is invariably an ex-racer with super-thin wheels. A walker like me, therefore, travelling hundreds of kilometres from the north to the south of France is a phenomenon most people find difficult to appreciate. The pilgrim, however, on an official GR footpath is a different matter.

It is Monday and everything in Blanzac is shut except a Bar/Restaurant in the main square overlooking the church. The owner, Mark, an Englishman, bought the business some

2 ½ years ago and starts by saying 'Well, I didn't expect to make any money when I came here'. He tells me there used to be a factory in Blanzac that employed 400 people but it closed 10 years ago and since then the village has been in decline. I note from where I am sitting that the shop fronts are shabby and the church, despite some fine early features, has long mossy stains on the west side which gets all the bad weather. By my table is a glass-fronted bookcase with all the household name English cookery books in it and plenty of not-so-obvious ones, so he clearly is interested in food. There are also some inscribed silver golf trophies, all from England. Mark is a hard-working northerner who cannot find reliable staff locally. There are plenty of people who drift in and out but no-one to give him the sort of support he needs. It is already 12:20 and customers are beginning to come in for lunch but the cook, who is good apparently, has still not turned up. This is quite normal and Mark has got used to doing all the preparation himself during the latter half of the morning. He says it is connected with the '35 hour working week' legislation which is producing a generation of work-shy workers. He wishes the cook had arrived on time this morning, however, because he has had to spend the first couple of hours of his day clearing up the flood which greeted him first thing after last night's storm. There is a serious problem with the roof but he has had to postpone the work on it.

The cook arrives ten minutes later with a luscious-looking girlfriend who does the rounds saying hello to all her friends in the bar. I note that the greeting round here is four kisses on alternate cheeks so it takes her a time to get round everybody. Meanwhile the cook has unsmilingly set to and this gives Mark the time to spend a moment or two with his guests. He appears to have a regular clientele and everyone gives the impression of knowing him well. He speaks rudimentary French and doesn't understand much of what the customers say but he serves a good lunch, presides over a jolly group of local people propping up the bar and looks happy. A sounder knowledge of the language would ease the process of integration considerably, I feel.

From where I am sitting I have a clear view of what is happening in the kitchen, and wish I hadn't. If anything is spilt on the side of the plate or bowl during serving, Mark runs his finger along, licks it, then repeats the operation before bringing the food out and placing it in front of the unsuspecting customer.

When I am still a couple of kilometres away I see tonight's *château* on some high ground looking enchanting in the warm afternoon sunlight. It is obviously very old and has a squat tower with slit windows on each corner. Eventually I reach the entrance to a kilometre-long rough driveway flanked on both sides by mature plane trees. It rained heavily overnight so I have to dodge some deep pot holes and steer my way round banks of mud. There clearly isn't much ready cash available to maintain the drive which is no doubt one of the reasons why they are reduced to running a dinner, bed and breakfast. When I rang to confirm, Monsieur said that since I was the only person staying tonight he would recommend a nearby restaurant for dinner, but as soon as he learned that I was arriving on foot he said he would put something together.

I find it difficult to announce my arrival. The main door on the south terrace has a rusty chain to one side that is attached to a bell half-way up the wall so I pull, then pull again, but no-one comes. I then set off to walk round the house looking for signs of life. Doors and windows are open with piles of ironing and signs of activity within but despite my shouts of 'Anyone at home?' nobody responds. I can hear a radio playing somewhere. I continue round to the stables where there is a builder high up a ladder repairing some of the stonework with a cement mix, and talking to him at ground level, my host.

'You are the first person to arrive here on foot', he says. 'Earlier in the summer we had an English couple in their 80s who arrived by bike after having done a round trip of 1200 miles through France. They showed me the milometer to prove it. When they came down to dinner they both looked immaculate and I asked them how it was possible to look so elegant when they were living out of panniers. But the English are like that'.

'Yes, we are', I reply, 'but please don't expect any elegance as far as I am concerned', thinking gloomily of my one-size-fits-all-man-made-fibre tee shirt and ultra lightweight flip-flops that I would be wearing later.

He shows me an elegant and airy drawing room and a dining room with an enormous table, then upstairs to my bedroom which has *St. Jacques de Compostelle* written on the door. My bathroom is in the round tower, access to which is through a very low doorway. I make careful note of this in case I have to negotiate it in the middle of the night. It is all very grand and from my perch on the lavatory at the top of the tower I can look due south through the slit window over my route tomorrow.

Monsieur joins me for drinks in the drawing room. He recommends cognac with tonic water which surprises me somewhat but I feel I must give it a try. I immediately wish I had opted for the gin. He tells me that in the high season they are always full, that guests normally dress for dinner but that I needn't worry about my informal attire, and anyway I am the only one staying tonight. I decide to enjoy myself. After all, it would be ridiculous trying to hide my flip-flops under the coffee table because he has already noticed them.

Madame looks sulky and ill at ease over dinner. For some reason they have put me at the head of the table which makes me feel that I am intruding somehow on their private lives so I feel almost obliged to say that I would not like to have paying guests because I couldn't handle the invasion of my privacy. This breaks the ice. He is a natural gentleman so doesn't admit it straight away but she, on the other hand, talks at length about how she hates living here and how the guests don't make her life any easier. He tells me of his flat in Paris and a house in Brittany both of which are rented out so they are obliged to spend the year here in the country.

'It is only the French who do not like the country; the English prefer the country to the town'.

Although he doesn't admit as much I suspect that he has a substantial inheritance tax bill to pay and is too attached to this house to let it go. Madame now says how much she would have preferred to marry into the Domecq family, live in Seville and spend her time on horseback. Her husband politely lets her have her say knowing that he is not in the same league as the Domecqs. Madame says 'merde' and repeats how much she loathes the invasion of their privacy and that when she drove past me on the road this morning she said to herself 'I bet that loony's the one who's coming to us later on today'. There ensue loud, angry whispers from Monsieur in the kitchen and when she comes back she spends the next 5 minutes apologising.

She is coquettish and very friendly over breakfast. Could I write a letter for her in Spanish to some Barcelona lawyers who came to stay in the summer and ask them to find their daughter a flat? She suggests one or two Spanish words which are wrong and which her husband knows to be wrong.

'Oh can't you just shut up for once Mister Know-All?' she says, her eyes blazing. Then to me: 'My only ambition is to learn fluent Spanish before I die. You know, I think I was a *sevillana* in a previous incarnation'.

Monsieur listens meekly to all this and says how much he would love to do what I am doing but cannot because there are too many ties on his time. In the meantime I am served two boiled eggs for breakfast 'pour vous gonfler' , which I think a rather good expression for it means 'to inflate you' rather than quite simply 'to fill you up'. Monsieur takes

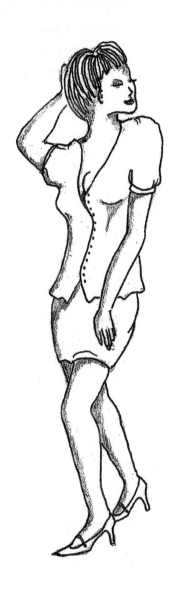

She is coquettish and very friendly over breakfast.

a photo of me with Madame (at her request) in front of the door.

'Oh do hurry up', she keeps saying. Then she grabs the camera and takes a few of me setting off down the pot-holed drive in the early morning mist. They both stand there waving till the mist swallows them up.

Spiders' webs spanning ditches and cobwebs covering whole fields glisten as the sun shines through the mist making them look as though they are made of glass. A crane takes off from a lake and I hear the whoosh of wings over my head then it disappears into the mist. Shapes loom in and out of my field of vision: here some cows floating on the meadow; in the next field a whole acre of bright orange pumpkins just being touched by the sun; up there on the slope men and women hand-picking grapes, their voices and the click of the secateurs sounding damp and muffled; suddenly, where a lane meets the road, a heavy wooden cross comes into view dripping onto a stone base. And so it continues until I reach Monmoreau with the mist hanging over the valleys and beginning to break up on the ridges. Early autumn bonfire smoke at the bottom of a valley rises white through the mist and turns blue when the sun catches it.

I plan to lunch in Aubeterre which is already being advertised on the side of the road as 'L'un des plus beaux villages de France'. I have been warned that the English have taken it over but that it is very beautiful and well worth a visit. Under no circumstances should I miss the monolithic church which is the largest in Europe and dates back to the 6th century.

The English start appearing miles before I get there, squinting at me through their windscreens. There are plenty of Parisians too who swerve out of my way at the last minute and gawp as they rush past. One woman, apparently on her own, bursts out laughing and points as she passes then I notice the children on the back seat who turn and stare through the back window. I hear English on the outskirts of the village, two women in neighbouring properties chatting over the garden fence. Out of one window comes a Radio 4 news bulletin. Adverts are mainly in English: 'Musical Evening'; 'Guided Tours'; 'Estate Agents'. A French woman in the car park with fluent English speaks loudly into a mobile 'phone: 'Please remind her we are meeting the owners at 2:30 this afternoon'. Somebody else in the street says to her companion: 'See you later'.

The main square looks very beautiful in the warm glow of the afternoon sunshine. The shop fronts are all original and in very good order; the pavements of fine stone slabs. There are three or four restaurants, each with a cluster of tables under the plane trees in the centre and many of them are already taken. I establish myself at a table and prepare for the moment when I remove my boots and allow my feet to find their normal shape and temperature again. This boot removal moment is one of the highlights of the long-distance walker's day and has to be relished like a fine wine but my concentration is disturbed by the veritable cacophony of English voices assailing my ears from all sides.

I hear whole English sentences in well-oiled raised voices reverberating off the pretty shop façades and houses. The loudest table is next to mine with three couples sitting in front of four empty bottles of wine although they haven't started eating yet. I take out notebook and pen and begin to scribble word for word what I hear being said all around me. All I can say is that this is an exact replica of what I heard between ordering my own lunch and its arrival at my table.

'I was in one of my two 1930 racers, both very good hill climbers. Angoulême's a fantastic circuit to drive on but I had the wrong tyres on, and I should have been twenty three, not sixty three, and my mind more alert. Liz was really worried. Thought I was dead, upside down and everything.' [loud guffaws]

'Retired surgeons don't operate in a horrid kind of way. I mean, I don't take limbs off or anything.'

'We got £900,000 for our house, and I don't buy steak here now. I buy lamb.'

'You're a Stoic? I went to St. Edward's and we used to play Stowe. Chrissie was at Cheltenham Ladies'.'

'He is the uncle of the man who married that bizarre songster woman, Madonna.'

'We can do the Daily Mail easy one on the back page but I don't want to torment myself with impossible puzzles.'

'She's a widow but she's in corking form and insists on paying her way but I can't handle that so I said give me 100 quid for a few nights' serious boozing.'

[Shakes the bottle to see if there's any left then shouts to the waitress]

'Deux encore bouteilles. We can always have a snooze later, can't we?'

'I have a brother who's terribly deaf. My hearing's fan-bloody-tastic. What was that you said?' [loud guffaws]

'She seems to think there's a part of England called Wales.'

'Poppy's flat is so amazing. It's got a 52' flat screen TV in the loo.'

It is now 2 pm and a workman digging the drains outside my restaurant warns the two waitresses that he is going to have to start the digger again.

'At least it'll drown out the bloody English' he says, and they all laugh.

The two waitresses begin to chat as I pay the bill and are entirely bowled over by the concept of my walk.

'So you're visiting all the villages from England down to south west France? That's amazing'. They examine my boots and sticks which are all beginning to show considerable signs of wear by now and ask for a quick calculation of how many kilometres I reckon I have covered in all, then stand and stare at me wide-eyed. 'Are you mad?' They have a point, I feel.

The lady charging an entrance fee at the 6th century monolithic church asks if I am a pilgrim and waves me on when I tell her about my walk. I enter a vast gloomy cavern significantly higher and more spacious than the average parish church and entirely made by chipping away at the living rock. I learn later it is 27 metres long by 16 metres wide. It is difficult to believe it was only discovered in 1958. Two sturdy rock pillars 20 metres high stretch from the floor up to the top of the cave. On the east side is an altarpiece, again carved out of the rock. The overall impression is initially so overwhelming that I have to stand leaning against the wall whilst I come to terms with this extraordinary space. The walls are black with damp but near the electric light bulbs are small green plants clinging to the rock. The floor is very damp and slippery. On the wall is a cross in bas relief standing beneath a shallow arch, both carved out of the stone. This main body of the church was originally believed to be 12th century until they discovered a 5th or 6th century baptismal font. To the west an arch leads to a separate 6th century chapel which is crammed full of open stone tombs, all empty now, similarly hollowed out of the rock. Behind one of the massive pillars is a steeply sloping path with occasional steps that rises right to the top of the church where there is a balustrade pierced in the rock through which the whole cavernous space can be seen. I feel so exhilarated by this place that my normally chronic vertigo, despite the unsteadiness afforded by my back pack and the slipperiness underfoot, virtually disappears. There is also a crypt on a lower level, reached by a steep path, with a low, vaulted roof, all blackened like the main church.

As I emerge into the sunlight I ask two men in white short-sleeved shirts and black ties my way out of the village, members of a religious sect with bundles of coloured pamphlets in their arms and a sense of urgency about them.

They direct me to the shopkeeper round the corner and walk briskly on.

7

La Dronne – La Dordogne

Just beyond Aubeterre is the boundary with the department of Dordogne and immediately roofs on the houses take on that typical Périgord look with the sudden downward slope, almost vertical at first, down to the eaves. People are more outgoing too and at last begin to proffer a 'bonjour' at the same time as me. It is still a fact that French children are taught at school to greet strangers with a cheery 'bonjour' and one of the big differences between England and France is that French people do take the trouble to greet fellow shoppers in shops. 'Bonjour Monsieur Dame' is what is normal but people of a certain old-fashioned elegance (lumped under the generic term *Vieille France)* insist on the less lazy and more correct 'bonjour Madame; bonjour Monsieur'. In England and north of Niort however, I had to initiate the conversation or we would have passed each other in stony silence so it is particularly good now on the Charente/Dordogne border to have my 'bonjour' cheerily returned. Up till now, apart from children, people have said nothing much in reply and only stared at me gloomily. Not even my fellow fresh air freaks, the cyclists, have been able to manage a nod, which I find odd because I feel there should be a sort of *camaraderie* between us.

For the very first time, just one kilometre from Festalemps, a lady in her garden giving me (correct) directions pronounces Festalemps with a very slight southern twang. She has just filled a trug with gleaming tomatoes, aubergines and peppers and is about to start on the beans. And now, again for the first time, I see someone approaching me along the road on foot. There is something about his slow, deliberate walk, the way he holds his head and his vacant stare that shows he is not normal. He stands stock still as I pass by, scrutinises me carefully, doesn't return my greeting and is still standing in the same place a minute or two later when I turn to look back at him.

Catherine and Philippe Legrand live in a lovely house through an old stone arch three metres behind the ancient rounded east end of Festalemps church. They have converted the outbuildings on two sides of the yard into *gîte* accommodation and installed a pool hidden behind a wall so it doesn't dominate the view as one comes through the gate. There are flowers cascading out of pots on all sides and a shady trellis. Through a space in the outbuildings is a wide rolling view east. She deals with every aspect of their tourist trade and tells me she has a policy of no keys or locked doors anywhere on the premises, including the bathrooms, and hopes that is all right. She also says that I am the second guest ever for whom she is prepared to make dinner, the first being a cyclist some years ago. She never prepares meals, other than breakfast, for motorised guests. She is a very no-nonsense, sensible woman presiding over a clean, tidy, well-run household in the midst of which her moping teenage daughter slumps like an old rag doll. She wants to 'doubler', or repeat this year at school, not helped by the teachers who are hardly setting the right kind of example to their charges by yet again going on strike throughout France the day after tomorrow. Catherine is visibly annoyed by this for her daughter has a pile of homework which she proposes not doing tonight because the teachers have said they won't collect it in the morning.

'How can you expect to do well if that is your attitude?' she says to the daughter, not wanting to appear too angry in front of me.

I offer to help with any English or Spanish work that may be outstanding but none has been set. While the daughter sits and eats grapes I tell Catherine about my lunchtime experience at Aubeterre and ask what effect the veritable hordes of English people have on the local population. She sums up:

'Not good. They arrive with no French language skills and make no effort to acquire any; they employ English builders, plumbers and electricians; they do their shopping in English expecting everyone else to understand; they stay in ghettoes and contribute nothing to the community.

Those that do, and there is one couple in Festalemps that have bothered to learn the language and involve themselves in what is going on, are respected and liked and invited into people's houses. Apart from that, it is two communities and the French don't like it'.

All this goes right over the head of the rag doll daughter who clearly is not at all affected by the British invasion but only wants to know the time of dinner. She slumps off out of sight.

Suddenly the kitchen door is flung open and Philippe (whom I have not yet met) bursts in stripped naked shouting 'Get me the vinegar, I'm covered in fleas', then he rushes out again calling 'Bonjour' to me, re-appearing in due course smelling of vinegar and displaying all the bites. 'They have bitten me everywhere', he says, 'everywhere' and looks earnestly at me through his John Lennon specs to make sure I have understood precisely where the offending fleas have been. As he dresses I learn he is a surveyor with a particular interest in old buildings and that he is 'passionate' about his work. He was clambering through the attic of an old building in the village moving a pile of wood to get a closer look at the beams when the fleas attacked him.

'Why on earth would fleas live in a pile of old wood?' I ask, 'they can't find much to eat there.'

'You don't need much to eat if you're a flea', says Catherine.

We now hear shouts from upstairs where Philippe has discovered the daughter slumped in front of the TV, not doing her homework.

'They have bitten me everywhere', he says, 'everywhere'.

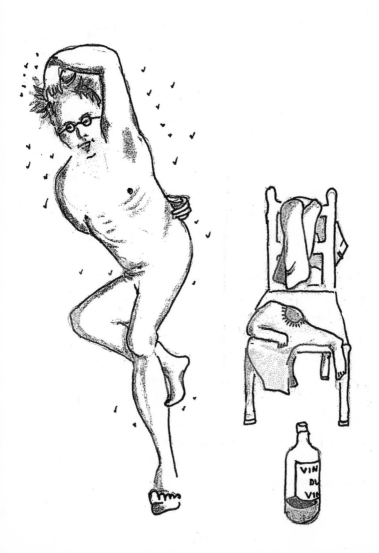

At breakfast Philippe tells us all that, when he went to get the bread this morning, the village baker confirmed that fleas do live in old wood and that he often has to hose down piles of logs with a mixture of water and bleach before being able to put them in his oven. This baker incidentally is Serge Bourland who wins the prize for the finest bread from St. Malo to St. Puy. He is head and shoulders above all the other bakers I come across throughout my journey. His bread is so renowned locally that his shop doesn't have a sign above it. You just have to know which door to push open.

Bread is another French sacred cow and again one should take great care before criticising it. It is after all present at every meal and because it is so light it can easily accompany a dish when a heavier English bread cannot. The French don't need to have cheese biscuits because their bread is not too filling at the end of a meal. We have all experienced warm, crunchy bread which is normally baked at the back of the *boulangerie*, arrives in the shop in top form and it's difficult not to break the end off on the way home. But in the vast majority of cases I think the deliciousness stops there. Most French people eat the bread produced by the local baker and never stop to question it, and yet most bakers buy in frozen dough and do no kneading on the premises. The result is a bread that is deceptively nice when warm and crusty but soon becomes chewy and tasteless. There is a growing number of *boulangers artisans* who make excellent bread in the old style but even they often do a bottom of the range *baguette* or *flûte* made with frozen manufactured dough to provide customers with a low price option. It is the case that most restaurants, *petits hôtels* and housewives in France buy this poor quality option for economic reasons and it is always blithely accepted. If one is walking long distances every day, however, the sustaining quality of the breakfast *baguette* and of the bread basket on the lunch and dinner table is something one notices. I can safely say that the poor quality option was the preferred choice of the majority of my hosts along my route, but today is the one stunning exception.

After the best *baguette* I have had for a very long time, Philippe insists on taking me to see the Romanesque church at Cumond which he describes as 'a unique marvel', so I can hardly refuse. There is another moment of absolute panic when we both get in the car and discover that it is crawling with fleas but we are out and have brushed each other down before any damage is done. Whilst Catherine goes off in search of the vacuum cleaner, we take the other car to Cumond, only a couple of kilometres away. The west door is indeed remarkable with a number of arches forcing the eye towards the door. Indeed, such is the perspective that one feels the urge to go right up to the door and enter the building. I have visions of the goodly folk of Cumond throughout the ages never missing their religious obligations because a medieval architect made it impossible for them ever to do so. The rest of the church is undistinguished and spoilt by a heavy-handed 19th century restoration which is why I walked straight past it yesterday. I meet Monsieur de Cumond, the Count emerging from his lovely old house surrounded by a high stone wall. He owns everything in sight and controls the keys to the church.

'He's very religious' says Philippe in a whisper, 'but (I like the 'but') he is very nice'.

Monsieur de Cumond, on learning what I am doing, tells me he has a friend who walked from Paris to Jerusalem.

'Much madder than me, then', I retort, which makes him smile.

It is another glorious morning and I am passing through dense woodland with beautiful dappled light coming from a sun which is still low in the sky. I can hear running water and pass some muddy ponds with many active pond-skimmers rushing about wildly on the surface. There is an occasional plop as a frog takes fright and jumps into the water. There are some clearings with cattle wearing bells that dong gently as I pass by. A couple of mushrooms have pushed the tarmac out of their way on the road surface about 20 cm from the verge and now stand proudly showing who is the stronger.

When the road plunges back into the woodland I can hear larger animals crashing about some way off and a pig-like squeal. I wonder what I would do if I came across a wild boar on the road, particularly a sow protecting her young, and decide that I wouldn't have much time actually to do anything. I practise my fierce stare and resolve to stare it out and stand as still as a statue in the hope it will ignore me and move on. The crashes grow louder. So far only one car has passed me and I have been on the road an hour.

If there is a boar out there I shall be entirely on my own. But these are fanciful thoughts which most people who have walked alone through dense woodland have often had and I am glad soon to see the wood give way to arable land as I near Echourgnac.

The church and the buildings here are disappointing in comparison with the splendours I have travelled through recently. There is, however, a bar into which I go for a glass of chilled Perrier. The owner is an old man sitting motionless behind the bar doing puzzles out of a magazine while someone else lays the tables for lunch. He asks the usual questions and gets all the usual answers but remains totally unfazed by my walk and returns to his puzzles. Today's Ouest France is on the bar and my horoscope foresees a definite slowing down in my progress: 'The brakes are being applied and you're going to slow down for a while'. How on earth can they possibly know that I am nursing a bad blister? It is as well that they reckon I have 'good morale' because I calculate that, all being well, I'll have finished my walk in six days.

Suddenly the old man puts down his puzzles and blurts out that in mid-August at seven in the morning, just after he had opened up, he saw a lone cyclist with a support car just behind displaying on the door a placard saying '4000 kilometres non-stop'. We both wonder if it can really have meant exactly what it said.

'Well it was in the following day's paper' says the old man, poking today's paper, 'so you've got to believe it'.

'But do you think non-stop means just that?' I ask incredulously, knowing that I am incapable of walking another step whenever I finally get to my day's destination.

'Well, you can feed and drink through a tube whilst cycling, and do *pipi*, but as for all the rest, *c'est pas évident*'.

I opt to provide no translation here. We spend some minutes calculating how many kilometres the lone cyclist could cover in 24 hours and how many days he could keep going without collapsing. In the end we are agreed it would be bad for one's health to attempt such a ride.

'*Courage*', he says as I leave. '*Courage* - only six days to go'.

I have discovered that whenever I leave my lodgings, a café or a restaurant, people tend to say 'courage'. This is the same word you would use to encourage a tennis player who has just dropped service, or a labourer digging a ditch on a wet day. Its real meaning is 'keep going; don't give up; keep at it', the implication being that you are involved in a physical activity that is not entirely enviable. Compare it with the English 'Have a nice walk' which you would say to a Sunday afternoon stroller as well as to a long-distance walker like me. The implication is that there is enjoyment to be had, and I am certainly enjoying every minute of this walk through France.

I find my walking poles are a source of great interest. One lady in her vegetable garden recently called out as I approached: 'On avance bien vite à quatre pattes' [you can walk really quickly on four feet]. Then one cyclist to another approaching me at speed and not realising that his voice was

'You can feed and drink through a tube whilst cycling, but as for all the rest, c'est pas évident'.

carrying: 'Regarde celui-là. Il roule à quatre jambes' [look at him bowling along on four legs].

The next hamlet is called La Vache Morte through which the lone cyclist must have cycled but no doubt he had his head down and didn't see the sign. I see it, however, and think gloomily of today's horoscope. There is a new villa on the outskirts of the hamlet with smart white gates and a gravelled drive. Suddenly I hear fierce barking and the gravel being kicked up by tiny feet. It looks like a Jack Russell so at first I am not too alarmed, but it is so small that it jumps easily through the bars of the gate and comes straight for me. Although all my attention is on the dog I can see through the corner of my eye a corpulent female figure in dressing gown and slippers standing on the drive observing the proceedings. Swinging my sticks just makes the dog angrier, but I have to swing them more and more vigorously because it is getting closer and closer to my ankles and I can see it has needle-sharp teeth. If the owner weren't there I would defend myself more physically but I don't want a lawsuit on my hands. Gradually I retreat up the road fighting a rearguard action against a tiny but formidable enemy whose commanding officer remains standing impassively, smiling on my misfortune. Did La Vache Morte get its name from a similar incident in the past, I wonder? Is this what the horoscope meant when it mentioned brakes being applied and me slowing down for a while? My loathing of small vicious dogs is well known but this incident takes it into an entirely new dimension. A bitten ankle at this stage could scupper everything.

My road now begins to wind downhill towards the curiously named St. Laurent des Hommes and beyond the village it continues steadily downhill as I get closer to the Dordogne. Someone has written *Je t'aime* in white paint on the road. Quite propitious I think, and it banishes all memories of the bad horoscope from my mind. Two male cyclists whizz into view.

'Bonjour Madame' they shout at me as they zoom past.

I hear giggles receding into the distance and catch a faint whiff of alcohol on the cool morning air. I rather enjoy the exchange as they are the only cyclists to have acknowledged my presence since I started out from St. Malo. I wonder if they are anything to do with the *Je t'aime* painted on the road about a kilometre behind me and half expect a return visit but my map instructs me to turn off the road. Probably just as well.

Pointing off this road is a sign to Cluzeau and I wonder whether the Pink Panther creator ever passed through here and adopted the name. I begin to compose a new Pink Panther script in my mind with Sellers and his girl ending up in the Hôtel Victor Hugo where I am heading tonight and then very suddenly and very unexpectedly the road ends. Admittedly it isn't much of a road, just a couple of metres wide and nothing has passed me in either direction for some time, but the map firmly states that it is there and that in a couple of kilometres it will reach a larger, busier road. I walk on south obeying my trusty compass down a track to a dilapidated farmhouse with the usual jumble of rusty abandoned cars and ancient machinery scattered outside. The map shows the house quite clearly with the original road going past it due south, but road, or anything like a road beyond the house there is not. There is an overgrown orchard and a long tangled hedge behind it but there isn't a path or even a trace of one. I go back to the house knowing that it is probably abandoned. Some grubby lace curtaining hangs crookedly inside a filthy window and the three steps up to the front door have grass growing out of the cracks. I am cheered, however, by the grimy shine on the huge door-knocker which informs me (I am still in my Pink Panther mode) that someone probably lives here after all. Not a sound comes from within. Perhaps after all it is one of those abandoned houses that peasant farmers use to house the pig so it is best to proceed with caution. I knock but my knuckles make very little noise on the thick old door. I think I hear 'Entrez' spoken by someone without a hint of surprise in their voice and yet I must be the first visitor here for a very long time. Perhaps it is just in my imagination, so I knock again. 'Entrez', slightly louder this time.

It is one of those front doors (you see them all over the south of France) that is not a single door but a double one and normally only one vertical half opens, the other half remaining firmly shut. Normally this half door would give me plenty of room to get into the house, but even after all this time I fail to reckon with my rucksack that increases my girth twofold and makes a smooth passage through the door impossible. In Inspector Cluzeau style therefore I push and strain feeling a complete idiot as a third, even louder 'Entrez' comes from within. When every muscle in your body is intent on getting you through a door there comes a moment when, despite yourself, you burst uncontrollably in. This I do and almost collide with the hapless, and no doubt by now terrified, dweller within. She is far from terrified but stands every inch as tall as me, 17 stone, at least 80 years old, and bearded. She is wearing a grubby black overall and worn out black carpet slippers and is standing in front of a grey sink drawing a chicken. The plastic tablecloth over time has become stuck to the top of the table and the pattern has worn white where the wooden planks meet beneath it. There is one solitary upright wooden chair. The room is filthy and exudes a background stench of warm guts and of damp soot from the fireplace. All this I notice in a split second and am immediately keen to leave so state my business. She tells me to go west (quite wrong – I need to go south constantly) and raises a flabby arm with a gooey hand at the end. Once again I fight with the door with her huge presence this time at my back. When I eventually stumble down the steps I feel obliged to follow her directions to the letter, and against my better judgement walk west, her eyes burning into the back of my head. I dismiss all speculation that she may have put some curse on me, though it is tempting.

This puts a few kilometres on my day. One lady tending her garden tells me cheerily that the D32 is 500 metres away. In fact it turns out to be nearer 5 kilometres. I am now on a long straight road aptly called the Chemin du Dry (my water has run out and I am parched). I ask a nubile 18 year-old girl on a bike where I am. She takes my map, turns it round and round (some people just don't have the spatial awareness), finds her own house with a little cry of triumph 300 metres away, shrugs and points me again west, but this time I just rely on the compass. When I eventually get to a crossroads with a cluster of road signs I can see where I am on the map. I have unwittingly made a huge detour and added many kilometres to my day's march.

When I finally get to the Hôtel Victor Hugo I discover much to my dismay that it is no more than a *brasserie* with a few rooms above. The bar downstairs is full of smoke and has sticky furniture and a tell-tale *buffet froid* cabinet up against one wall. I now know from experience precisely what dinner and breakfast will be like and wait for Madame to wipe her hands on a damp grey towel. The stairs with their old bleach stains on the worn carpet are a fitting precursor of what is to come. Yet again I am in a room that is in urgent need of a refit. The plastic furniture is cracked and sticky like the bar downstairs and nothing works in the bathroom. The basin tap leaks permanently, the shower door doesn't fit and the bathroom floor, together with the splashed water, slopes towards the door, which explains the half circle of yellowing carpet that reaches as far as the bed. Madame is nevertheless a jolly soul and wishes me a 'bonne installation' before taking her leave.

When I eventually sink on to the bed I think not of Peter Sellers but of Hugo himself and his collection of poems with the somewhat daunting title *Les Châtiments* (Punishments). There ought to be a standard issue copy on all the bedside tables in this dreary place that bears his name.

Funny to think, however, that a book with such a title could contain a verse as uplifting as:

'Mangeons, buvons, tout le conseil!
Heureux l'ami du raisin mûr,
Qui toujours, riant sous sa treille,
Trouve une grappe sur son mur
Et dans sa cave une bouteille!'[1]

I decide that there is nothing for it but to take his advice. Despite my fatigue it is worth walking another half kilometre to the village restaurant which must be better than the *brasserie* and over a memorable dinner I order a good bottle of the local Ste. Foy la Grande (Grand Vin de Bordeaux), a snip at €11. The last half of my day recedes into the distance.

---

[1] Let's eat, let's drink, that's my advice! Happy the friend with ripe grapes, who, as he laughs under his arbour, can always find a bunch growing against the wall, and a bottle in his cellar.

8

La Dordogne – La Lot

I start off the next morning with the Dordogne just in my sights through the mist and eventually cross it by the narrow road bridge at Gardonne which is an undistinguished, somewhat ugly place full of early morning traffic and people bent on getting to work on time. I am now on a footpath on which I will spend the best part of the day heading due south in glorious warm sunshine towards the heart of the Bergerac wine country. Soon I am in the midst of the vines opening and shutting like a fan as I advance (Lorca's image, not mine), and they are busy with the harvest here too.

Saussignac is an important centre of wine production according to the large municipal map that stands opposite the hotel (closed for repairs so no chance of a cold drink). There are between twenty and thirty different *châteaux* in the commune, one or two named quite simply after the grape variety (*Château Merlo; Château Tannagras*) while other names concentrate on the possible effect that their product might have on the drinker (for example *Château Pissepetit*). At the bottom of the map is a quotation from Rabelais about the monks of nearby Monestier which is of some interest to me as Monestier is next stop on my route. Apparently these monks are 'good drinkers of Saussignac'. A Rabelaisian monk would indeed be a heavy consumer but the monks I actually come across in Monestier show no signs of whooping it up. I pass four young men in brown habits that may be Franciscans although they don't have the hood or the knotted cord. All four are painfully thin and have shaved heads. Certainly the real Franciscans I came across in my youth were what Rabelais would call 'bon viveurs' and had the girth to accompany it. These Monestier monks smile broadly enough as we pass on the path and although they can't manage a 'bonjour' (perhaps they are foreign?) their body language makes it clear that they are at least happy.

I am surprised very shortly after this while still in the commune of Monestier to come across a different sort of monk altogether wearing dark brown pantaloons down to his ankles. In fact it is the pantaloons I see first as he is bending over with a pair of secateurs in his hand, bald scalp, oriental features, nose a few inches off the ground, about to cut a twig. He starts when he hears me and takes a time to recover his composure. I am not lost so have no need of directions (my compass has just reassured me I am heading in the right direction on a woodland path), but I think I will ask him to confirm my way to Puyguilhem because I am keen to engage him in conversation. The poor man has no French but points east down another path, trembling and trying to hide his secateurs in his clothing. Perhaps I caught him about to commit a dreadful act. I know that certain eastern religions find harming life in all its forms unacceptable and I caught him at it. When I turn round and look back he has disappeared.

Almost immediately on my right I see an eastern-shaped roof covered with traditional French *tuiles romaines* rising above the trees and fixed on what looks like an old stone farmhouse, then a lake with some very superior jet-black geese with red crests, then a deer park surrounded by a high fence. Just next to it half a dozen white goats, some donkeys and a mule in the same field. All this probably belongs to the monastery. Just in the folds of the hill on the top of which stands imposingly the village of Puyguilhem, there is a domed wooden structure ready to have a cover thrown over it to turn it into a shelter. I am so full of monks by now I think it might be a place where a hermit might go. I do know that sometimes the urge to leave the bosom of a monastic community without abandoning it altogether can be very strong.

On the edge of the wood, just under the very last trees before I start my ascent, is an old farm cart filled with vine stakes. Something about it, the play of the afternoon light through the trees, the fact that it is fixed in a horizontal position and not just casually parked, makes it seem like an artist's installation.

The Hotel des Vieilles Pierres in Eymet reminds me curiously of a place where we stayed at Alter do Chão half-way up the Amazon. An extraordinary leap for me from today's walk with all its fine wine and foreign monks back to the crushing heat and the loud whir of the straining air conditioning unit in our room that could only bring the temperature down to about 30 Centigrade. We looked out over a small courtyard with parrots flying around a vast cage under a couple of palms. A far cry indeed from this well-ordered, spotlessly clean room with radiators for the winter and a view over a similar courtyard dominated not by parrots but by sparrows screeching under an ancient walnut tree. It's about 25 degrees outside here so only a bit sticky, and the clouds are beginning to gather. I fear the good weather is going to break.

'Je vous envoie mille millions de baisers d'Aymet' (I send you thousands and thousands of kisses from Eymet). With these very words in 1588 the future king Henri IV signed off a letter to his mistress Diane d'Andouin. He obviously thought as well of the place as he did of her. Eymet is certainly pretty, but like Aubeterre, entirely overrun by the British. Here too the first language spoken is English. This doesn't matter too much in the bar in the main square because the owner either is English, or speaks the language fluently. He's certainly got a sense of humour because just inside the door is a hidden step which trips up everybody who comes in. On the walls are notices advertising goods and services, all in English, with strips at the bottom containing the 'phone number so if you are interested you tear off a strip and take it with you. Somebody is offering to buy and sell houses, explain French inheritance law, what to do in the event of a death, how to import a car or caravan, and finally French classes (all levels catered for) once a week in a private house. I look in an estate agent's window just in order to compare prices between here and the area around St. Puy, and immediately on the pavement next to me is a smart middle-aged Englishwoman who asks me (in English of course) what sort of place I am looking for. To be fair, I certainly look very eccentric and English, and no self-respecting Frenchman would dare wander round a town looking as dishevelled as me (flip-flops, one-size-fits-all-man-made-fibre tee shirt, and a decided limp from a swollen knee joint), but to be addressed thus in the middle of rural France throws me somewhat.

I then meet a Frenchman who is dressed almost as badly as me, a kindred spirit at last, trying to fix a mini motorbike on to the rack at the back of his campervan. He has just bought it for a mere €80 and is delighted with his purchase. I must say it looks very fine indeed. It weighs nothing, folds up neatly, would fit easily into a car boot and would very happily cover the last few kilometres back to St. Puy in about an hour or two. I don't make an offer although I am sorely tempted because the sky is now dark with rain clouds and the forecast is very poor.

I wake up to heavy rain and a strong southerly wind so am forced to climb yet again into my wet-weather clothes that so far have served me quite well, but I have to admit that with St. Puy so close now I could do without another whole day of this sort of thing. Other people seem comfortable in waterproof trousers and storm jacket complete with hood but I much prefer an umbrella and trilby to what is described in Millets as 'survival clothing'. I decidedly don't like wearing my hood although I realise it is an absolute must in poor weather like today's. There are a number of reasons for this: first, it plays havoc with my hearing. The sides make a rhythmic swishing noise in my ears as I walk along which I cannot get used to so I find myself constantly looking left into the ditch for what could be a large slithery creature, or over my right shoulder for an approaching car. And then when I turn my head to look either left or right my hood does not respond to this movement so I spend a lot of time looking at the inside edge of the hood that blanks out all further vision. I pass a barking dog, think it is way behind me, but in fact it is at my heels about to sink its fangs into my legs. The noise of the rain pelting down on my hood is reminiscent of tyres scrunching on gravel so I walk unsteadily on the grass verge in order to give the non-existent car behind me plenty of room. The hood does unpleasant things to my hair too, rather akin to stroking hair backwards, so that when I finally pull the hood away from my head my hair is tufted and actually aches as I try pushing it back to where it should be.

The bad weather hits me fully frontally. I can't see a horizon through the low cloud and driving rain so I concentrate on people's gardens which, so I have noticed, always seem to be at the front of the house. The garden boundary, be it a fence or a leylandii tree hedge, is immensely significant in France probably because it makes a man think he really is *chez soi*. I know such hedges exist in England and are often the subject of bitter disputes but I think they only very rarely completely surround the property. The fully-fledged leylandii hedge that, apart from the entrance gate, entirely surrounds one's property, is a peculiarly French invention. Within the boundary things grow in geometrical straight lines: a row of red flowers, then a row of blue, then yellow, each plant strictly 20 cm the one from the other. All patches of grass are dotted with pot-grown pine or cypress trees either plonked, which makes mowing difficult, or stuck right next to an offensive electricity pole.

The English cottage garden with its riot of forms and colours spilling over the path and climbing over the front door has never caught on in France maybe because the French don't spend much time actually in the garden. You see plenty of tables and chairs on sheltered terraces where warm weather dining takes place but here the focus of attention is the stomach and not the feast for the eyes that could be afforded by a well-planned garden. The neatest and most pleasing gardens I have come across so far are the *potagers* or vegetable gardens with long rows of produce growing sturdily in weed-free soil. One doesn't see vegetable patches very often in England because they are normally hidden from view round the back, but in France what is for the table is on display for all to see right at the front of the house. This means that many houses stand bleakly with few, if any, climbing plants to break the impact of the walls.

In such a culture reconstituted stone statuettes have an important rôle to play. Some people go in for gaily-painted dwarves but only as a daring stab at internationalism. They are much more fond of the reconstituted pure white stone figurine that can be found in every French garden centre. There is a veritably huge variety available and they dominate a large majority of French gardens: gnome (un-painted) crossing his legs and perched on a toy well; gnome with wheelbarrow full of flowering plants; gnome fishing out of an ornamental pond; gnome chasing a butterfly; gnome driving a cart (more flowering plants) pulled by two shire horses. Then there are reconstituted white stone donkeys with panniers full of real twigs; a miniature stone wine press (yet more flowering plants); rustic, fresh-faced children, the girl always with a frilly fringe to her dress, the boy with a floppy hat frozen in full romp round the garden; blissfully happy life-sized girl and boy playing inside a stone tube; ducks with expanded backs that hold different coloured pebbles or seasonal flowers; a huge stone snail in a flower bed; a fairy-tale bambi looking pretty amid half a dozen carefully planted silver birch trees in the 'wild' corner of the garden; and (surely this wins first prize) two 'black' slaves (white actually) holding umbrella stands in the porch.

Standing tall among all these is that peculiarly French invention, the pre-fabricated barbecue. There are a number of designs available in DIY supermarkets and all, broadly speaking, are identical with minor variations depending which supermarket you go to. Once erected they are permanent and remain to delight the eye throughout the year. They are all easy to use with the fire at waist level (no bending down allowed outside) and they have been covered with standard issue cream-coloured pebbledash which is supposed to blend with the environment and the surrounding buildings but which in fact screams at you as you pass by. Most have red brick edgings with a space for wood underneath the cooking slab. In fact these spaces are rarely used for wood (the jarring on the eye would be less if they were) because most people use barbecue coal out of a brightly coloured sack which is then stored in full view in the wood space. To crown it all (literally) is the chimney (more pebbledash, more bricks) that diverts the smoke and the smell of grilling meat up and away before they have the chance of reminding the cook and the cooked-for that they are cooking and eating food in the open air.

The following morning is bright and sunny but I have the problem of damp clothes that did not dry overnight in front of my window because it rained till very late. I leave my hotel therefore with a full range of clothes dangling from my back pack and oscillating merrily as I get into my stride. I wear my pants yet again on my sleeve and attract plenty of odd looks, pointed fingers and raucous laughter from a rowdy group of teenage boys waiting for the school bus. But I am fearless now and stride manfully past them.

I am used to people in passing cars looking at me with a mixture of surprise and disdain. Women tend to smile a 'poor-chap-can't-be-much-fun-walking-all-that-way' sort of smile while their man grips the wheel and positively scowls. Perhaps they look upon this stick-swinging vagabond as a threat to their own masculinity, and they all look disapproving. Single women demurely remain impassive although one in Deux Sèvres, emerging from her long access road on to mine, did raise a hand in greeting. I have been offered one lift (not accepted of course) by a single very beautiful lady in her late twenties with purple streaks in her hair in the middle of a heavy downpour. The best by far are the young who give me the thumbs up, plenty of toots on the horn and 'Ohhh' shouted out of the window as they speed past with their loudspeakers thumping. Sometimes I can hear their horn tooting for a minute or two.

Between Hautes Vignes (there's something very basic about the toponymy round here in that this village is on the top of a high hill and there are vines all around) and Clairac is the very beautiful small Romanesque church of Sainte Marthe. It is unusual because it has a new roof, restored stonework on the walls and a smart new oak door on which is pinned a note from the *Mairie* saying that people are very welcome to visit but could they please keep quiet in this place of worship. Predictably, however, it is shut but the outside is memorable enough including the cluster of robust, well-established cypress trees looking very good in the churchyard. They are the tree of the dead and serve their purpose beautifully when properly located.

It is doubly exciting just a couple of kilometres further along the road to come across another small Romanesque gem of a church in the same style and in as good order, but like Sainte Marthe's it is firmly shut. I love the style of pierced belfry with each bell hanging in its own little arch and I have seen examples all the way through France. It is such a shame when a church is in a woeful state of disrepair and I have passed quite a number over the last weeks. I suspect these two churches were funded by a local group of volunteers, something that one is seeing more and more often throughout the country. A church after all is the most striking and endurable building in any community and many are of considerable architectural merit. Perhaps the whole process of restoring them to their former glory will increase curiosity and entice greater numbers of people to pause and wonder why and how they come to be there. I am always struck by the enormous degree of faith that must have inspired the creation of these buildings in the first place, not merely the faith of the medieval noblemen who financed the project but also the unquestioning acceptance of both the craftsmen who built them and the local community.

9

La Lot – La Garonne

The next day I start from Clairac which is prettily reflected in the river Lot. Older houses here are built of flat Toulouse-style bricks and large grey pebbles no doubt taken from the river and they all have *tuiles romaines* on their roofs. It's a great day: the sun is shining and God is in his Heaven until all of a sudden two enormous Alsatians, tails stiff and hackles a mile high, burst through a factory entrance and come straight at me. I am on a busy road on the outskirts of Clairac about to negotiate a roundabout so I am cut off by heavy traffic on one side and mad dogs approaching fast on the other. I think they must have been beaten with a stick at some stage because as soon as I raise mine they back off growling angrily, fangs flashing in the early morning sun. I hate to imagine what would have been the outcome if they had got to me but I would almost certainly have had to postpone the rest of the walk, and that would have been particularly galling as I calculate I have only three days' walking left. I wonder how many pilgrimages have come to an abrupt halt in a violent way such as this from medieval times up to the present. It forces me to think yet again that there are still many unchained dogs to walk past and fast-moving vehicles to dodge and that it is far too early to become complacent. I might well be getting closer but I've had my fair share of unpleasant surprises and there may well be more in store.

As I move further away from the river, the pebbles give way to local grey stone which I find depressing and not at all as nice as our honey-coloured stone further south which looks pretty good even in rain and quite stunning in full sun. Local builders in recent years have tried to cheer things up by using white cement toned down with ochre, but the grey and the ochre don't mix. Many houses in the depths of the country, despite still being lived in, are in very bad repair and some are quite dilapidated. My impression is that this region is just waiting for an injection of new life and that it will come as soon as Parisians and foreigners discover it. Sadly, there probably isn't enough local money to achieve this so eventually the region will go the way of all the others and prices will rise way beyond the reach of local people. The locals should be buying houses now while they still can but in the past they haven't had to think so far ahead.

Something that I haven't fully appreciated before is that certain French country people appear never to throw away a rubber tyre. I have noticed both in the north and the south, and this part of the south in particular, that an old tyre is often recycled as a cheap form of flower pot. The French are fond of flower pots, in fact many French flower gardens depend very heavily on pots, so in many respects the tyre that doesn't pass the MOT is a long-lasting, frost-free alternative. Once you start looking out for them you notice the differences. They range from ordinary unadulterated black rubber tyres dumped unceremoniously outside the front door, filled with earth followed by the plant of the moment, to much more elaborate designs. Some are painted white; others are white with red treads picked out all the way round; others (and these are very arty) have been cut in such a way that a row of rubber triangles, painted whichever colour you please (the *tricolore* is the most popular), stand erect around the top. I go past a Lebanese cedar today which, judging by its girth, is at least fifty years old, and has been planted in the middle of a tractor tyre (painted white, no fancy cut-outs). It is odd to think that the tyre will outlive the tree.

Galapian is a pretty *bastide* village, though not a patch on Fourcès or Larressingle in the Gers. Its war memorial is covered with names from both wars with often the same families mentioned and is topped by a life-size statue of a French infantryman recently painted from head to toe in the brightest colours as if he's just been made up for a performance of *Journey's End*. No doubt he will weather in time but at the moment he is quite resplendent and this attempt to bring him to life forces one to pause for a moment and reflect. I have seen one other painted soldier like this on a war memorial, in St. Michel Mont Mercure, the highest point in La Vendée.

I climb up and up into the hills and then down again to Port Sainte-Marie where at last there is a bar open. The Madame eyes me disapprovingly as I remove my backpack and reveal the sweaty back of my shirt. I make some anodyne comment about the weather, that it's warmer here than in the north from where I have walked, then watch her eyes and mouth open wide. She says she's had walkers in here before but only day trippers. How can I possibly have come all that way? Why on earth am I doing it? I do wish people wouldn't ask really difficult questions like these. I can hardly reply 'Because I wish to know myself', for this straightforward, hard-working lady wouldn't know what I was talking about. So I reply 'Parce que', the French equivalent of 'Oh I just am, that's why' and feel thoroughly cross with myself for not making more of an effort. Her reply is a reassuring 'Eh, mais c'est pas évident' ('There's no need to be modest, that's quite an achievement') and she warmly wishes me 'courage' as I leave. She sets me thinking. Tomorrow I cross the Garonne; the day after tomorrow my walk is over so this is the time to take stock and determine what I have learned about myself during the last few weeks.

Embarking aged sixty all alone on a long walk such as this should have allowed me to do a bit of self-purging and learn at last who I really am and how I can best understand why I am part of this complex world. During the walk I have found myself concentrating for virtually the first time on my strengths and dismissing my weaknesses as a waste of precious time. How many sexagenarians nowadays are still married to the same person and blissfully happy to boot with three remarkable children each making their way in the world? A happy and united family is a rare and striking achievement in itself.

'Know Thyself' it said on the temple of the Delphic Oracle. I think I must know myself a little better now that I have almost finished this crazy venture but I am not over-impressed because I have learned nothing very attractive about myself. All the weaknesses and failings which I know I had at the beginning and which I pushed beneath the surface are still there and periodically come to hit me with a vengeance. I would like to think that I have become a little more tolerant and a little less judgemental but in fact I haven't. I have certainly discovered that there is much more good in the world than I thought and that there is good in the most unlikely people. That may sound a *cliché* to some but it means something to me. Many of those I have come across over the past weeks have taught me about the scope for improvement that is in every one of us and I would certainly like to think that one of the many benefits of my walk is that I wear something more noble than a pair of damp underpants on my sleeve.

I wouldn't have started this if I didn't think I had enough stamina to finish but I can sense after a good month on the road that my energy levels are nearing their limit. Of course I will finish; I am far too proud not to finish. I am ready too for a bit of companionship after such a prolonged period of self-imposed solitude and it will be a luxury to share meals and a glass of wine again with family and friends. All the time at the back of my mind is a niggling little pulse which I try to ignore but it keeps coming back. What next? Where next? A walk like this through Spain, despite all my current aches and pains, is beginning to sound irresistible.

10

La Garonne - La Gèle

It is a great moment when I cross the last of the great French rivers on my route, the Garonne, and enter the pretty little town of Bruch with its ancient stone buildings and a very fine small statue of the Virgin and Child above the west door of the church hidden behind some cunning iron work to keep the pigeons off. Just the sort of statue I'd love to have on my desk. I leave a busy road behind me and begin to see more gentleness in the landscape and some wide views but very, very few signs of habitation.

Fieux is a pretty little place perched on a hill with an impressive medieval stone building (now the *Mairie*) and corner turret overlooking my way south. There are the inevitable noisy dogs high up on a bank behind a fence but the fence soon runs out and in a moment one of them is snarling charmingly at my ankles. I wave my trusty sticks but they don't have much effect (clearly this dog has been well looked after) so I stand stock still and wait for it to calm down. 'Couché!' said sternly (the equivalent of 'Down, Rover, down!') seems to have some effect and, thank goodness, soon his tail begins to wag in a friendly fashion. In fact he stays with me at a safe 25 metre distance for up to 3 kilometres and might come the whole way if I encourage him. In the end I have to stand still, face him and tell him firmly to go home (in both languages for emphasis). He stands and looks at me for a long time as I move off whilst checking every ten seconds that he isn't following me and then finally he makes his mournful way back across the fields. All he wants is a bit of companionship and, that rare thing in France, a walk.

It is impossible to calculate the number of dogs with their owners that I would have come across had I walked as far as this in England along quiet country lanes. The extraordinary fact is I haven't seen one person walking a dog since St. Malo but I have been past literally hundreds of dogs either chained up to a stake, enclosed in a fenced run or shut in the front garden. All go completely berserk as I pass by and set off all the other dogs in the vicinity. Most of them wag their tails whilst creating this dreadful din; a small number don't, however, and look absolutely terrifying with their raised hackles, bulging eyes and glinting fangs.

I am approaching the centre of the village when I first hear her harsh rasping voice shout 'Viens' ('come on') with that southern twang that inserts a 'g' at the end of the word. 'Vieng…vieng…vieng…vieng'. My immediate thought is that she has detected my approach and wishes to grab hold of her dog before it jumps on me. I grasp my sticks more firmly in case the disobedient beast decides on the spur of the moment to direct all its energy into protecting mistress from this intruder. There is a wholesome smell of soup in the air and it has gone midday. As I round a bend I see them, but there is no dog, merely an old man well into his nineties who has just arrived and is standing in the drive by his ancient Renault 4 trying to fold his pullover, taking too long. Madame (probably his daughter) is keen to get on with lunch and continues shouting 'vieng' again and again at him. Neither of them sees me, for they are intently looking at each other, one keen to stick to her busy schedule and be back in the office by 2 pm, the other bemused, confused, locked into the timeless rhythm of the aged.

I move on to Francescas. At last the building stone is white with a tinge of honey and the village looks as though it has always been prosperous. Baskets of flowers hang from walls and there are potted plants at each door. A few market stalls are doing a brisk trade and shoppers call greetings to each other across the square. There is a cluster of expensive cars outside the restaurant and a group of customers talking loudly on the terrace. As I leave the village I know I am three kilometres away from the Lot et Garonne boundary with the Gers. Tomorrow, all being well, I should finally arrive at my destination but it would take just one angry dog or one careless driver to scupper this.

The difference between the *départements* of Lot et Garonne and the Gers is very noticeable very early on. Here is a working farm on the side of my road with two superb old stone-built chicken houses each with a ceramic chicken perched on the apex of the roof and each with a small pigsty door at the side. Now suddenly farms are proper homesteads with all the shutters thrown open, red, yellow and blue flowers in pots by the front door, women in dressing gowns (I started at 7:30 am) removing dead leaves and watering. There is a substantial house on each hilltop and even the more humble dwellings down here on the road have a solid, well-built look about them as if they are houses built on a full stomach. Having seen comparatively few big houses since the Dordogne I now go past three *châteaux* in one morning. This is 100 Years' War country. The views are wide, the horizon tens of kilometres away and I walk under a vast sky offering a whole range of different sorts of weather: great charcoal streaks dousing a distant hill with rain; in the middle ground a hill-top church lit by brilliant sunshine; dark, threatening rain clouds above, more blue-black than dark grey.

The great square towers of La Romieu loom into view with the long ogival windows of the *collégiale* in between. There is the usual cluster of tourists in the cloister and the buzz of chatter at the café tables under the arcade in the square. Opposite, outside the *Mairie*, is the bust of 14th century Angéline with her cats' ears and slanting cats' eyes. From an early age this local girl displayed considerable fondness for cats and legend has it that, as the years went by, she began to look more and more like her feline companions. In 1344, after a harsh winter and a rain-sodden spring when the crops couldn't be sown, the starving villagers were reduced to eating their cats to stay alive. Fortunately, Angéline's house was right on the edge of the village so she could keep hers safely in the attic, letting them out at night to hunt. When the harvest was plentiful again much of it was consumed by rats who had multiplied during the absence of cats and it was at this point that Angéline saved the day by releasing all hers who were only too pleased to rid the village of the tiresome rodents. Now there are cats sculpted out of stone dotted all over La Romieu, sitting on ledges, sleeping on window sills, crouching on gateposts, the idea of Maurice Serreau, a sculptor, who wanted to immortalise the legend in stone. Today La Romieu is a busy, thriving place on the *chemin de St. Jacques* so is visited by large numbers of pilgrims throughout the year on their way to Condom and beyond into Spain. How many of them, I ask myself, see the cats and wonder why they are there.

In June 1944, exactly six hundred years after Angéline delivered her fellow villagers from starvation, French, Spanish and English members of the *Résistance,* who must already know the war is almost won and that they are tantalisingly close to returning to their families, doggedly fight German troops that have been sent from Auch to crush the active cell that for two years has been secretly based at Castelnau sur l'Auvignon. Around twenty Spaniards are there to fight the Fascism they tried unsuccessfully to defeat in their own country during their Civil War. It is a decisive and bloody battle and the Germans, better armed, manage to take the village. A Frenchman fills the medieval stone tower with explosives which go off and inflict heavy casualties as the Germans enter the village but they go on to destroy everything, razing houses to the ground. There is now an impressive and moving memorial with the many names of the Spanish dead picked out in gold just a few feet away from the tower with the gaping hole still visible blown out of its side. The building is dangerous and cannot even be entered nowadays.

The village looks normal enough now with some of the new houses built on the ruins of the old. One or two of the houses nearest the tower are now rented out as *gîtes* and I hear German spoken as I walk past. For all its faults the European Community has successfully brought together old enemies who can now live in peace side by side, and that can only be a good thing. There is a school attached to the *Mairie* with a bench under a tree where tired pilgrims can sit and rest. Just 50 metres further on where the *chemin de St. Jacques* comes up a steep slope and hits the main village street is a stone *calvaire* with a pile of white stone pebbles at its base, left by pilgrims as they complete another stage of the long walk to Santiago. This is a quiet place but for me too full of violent memories and I leave by the same road up which not so long ago came a column of soldiers obeying deadly orders whilst the unsuspecting people of Castelnau were getting on with their daily lives.

I press on to Blaziert standing proudly on its steep hill, the two access roads lined with ornamental cherry trees for a good kilometre before reaching the main archway, with the white church spire pointing up to the wild sky. And now the road winds up and down gentle hills and small valleys past the delightful Romanesque church at Roquepine built literally on the rock at the highest point with well-tended flower beds on either side of the path leading to the main door.

I take a photograph of St. Puy as soon as I can see it standing on its hill three kilometres away, the church tower oddly lower than the dominant *château*. St. Puy, a corruption of the Latin *summum podium,* means literally 'on top of the hill' and in medieval times had more gates, and therefore more importance, than Auch, the big thriving town some 30 kilometres away. There is new building along this stretch too and a couple of very ugly modern barns so the view is no longer uninterrupted, but it is still magnificent in a sudden burst of brilliant sunshine and many birds are singing. It is not quite the pilgrim's first sight of Santiago but it's an emotional moment. The road dips and winds through fields past Terre Blanche farm, a major producer of *foie gras* and *spécialités gersoises*, and past some fine houses with enticing little towers that used to serve as *pigeonniers,* then it climbs up towards the cemetery and comes into the village at its highest point. The main dwellings are ahead and below along three or four streets that dip sharply away from the *château* and lead to the main square with its busy bar-restaurant (it is just midday as I arrive), chemist's, hairdresser's, baker's, butcher's and general stores. It is no longer the somewhat drab, grey place that it used to be when we first came here 25 years ago. Ancient stonework and timbers have been exposed on some of the façades, the post office and *Mairie* have been repointed with white cement and warm, ochre-coloured local sand, and the largest house (apart from the *château*) is now a shell being painstakingly restored by a famous son of St. Puy who has made it in a French television soap opera. I say 'bonjour' to all the familiar faces sitting by their doors on stone benches and they can't fathom why I should be walking with a backpack and a couple of sticks. They normally know me as the Englishman with the bright red 2CV posting a fistful of letters into the village box before driving off again down the hill beyond the village limits and into the very heart of the countryside beyond.

'Alors, ça a marché, la marche?' asks one old man, not realising why I find it so funny. 'Did the walk go well?' goes no way towards capturing the pun of the original.

With just three kilometres to go I can hardly believe that I have come all this way. A far cry indeed from medieval times when pilgrims set off map-less from Winchester and hardly expected to return safely. I have read in one of the guides that they underwent the most incredible hardships, one of which was to be invariably eaten alive by horse flies when they got to the Landes, just south of Bordeaux, and alarmingly close to my route. In

'Alors, ça a marché, la marche?'

those days they had regular robbers and mad dogs to fend off, plus the plague and a host of other dangers. I have been quite prepared for robbers and I have had my tussles with dogs but I have also had to cope with modern plagues such as relentless traffic, exhaust fumes and ring roads, not forgetting cars driven fast by drunken youths along lonely country lanes brandishing pistols. I have pretty well worn out a pair of new boots that used to have thick rubber soles with deep treads, and I have just put the seventh and eighth ferrules on my walking poles.

One needs to be physically as well as mentally prepared for a walk such as this. It just isn't easy to switch suddenly from a so-called normal existence to one which involves very early rising and, one hopes, huge breakfasting followed by five or six unremitting hours of walking. Most people have undertaken one long walk of twenty or twenty five kilometres in their lives, but few have done it relentlessly, in fair weather or foul, day after day for some weeks. In the end my adrenalin took over so I am able finally to reach my goal but not without a certain degree of discomfort.

The last 32 days appear to have passed in a flash but I have had my fair share of blisters and aching muscles mainly because I made an elementary mistake at the planning stage by taking a ruler and measuring 25cm (1cm = 1km) on the map between each stopping place. This was a mistake because the ruler does not reflect the many bends and turns on the road, and occasionally I found myself doing more than 32 kilometres (20 miles) per day. I had often done a 30 kilometre walk in the past and thought not much more of it because there was all the time in the world to recuperate afterwards. Had I covered a maximum of only 20 kilometres per day on this walk I would have found things a lot easier.

I feel I should also have incorporated many more rest days into the schedule. I needed these more and more as time went on for I did begin to slow down. At first I was able to spend most of the time every day walking at an average speed of 6 kilometres per hour, but after 10 days or so I could only keep this up in short bursts, and towards the end my speed often dwindled to 4 kilometres per hour. My walking day therefore lengthened over time. There is not much I could have done about all this apart from embark on such a journey when I was a good deal younger, but other demands made that impossible. My physical body may have got tired but, now that I have achieved what I set out to achieve, I find the spiritual uplift highly rejuvenating. I am striding along oblivious to aches and pains, delighted that as from tomorrow I'll be able to take things a lot easier.

My thoughts turn to the house that awaits me, the house that inspired this walk in the first place. There is nothing at all grand about it. Proust would describe it as a house in which one can 'vivre petitement'. It is what an estate agent would call *une fermette* although we have greatly increased the size by converting the large stable into extra rooms. The whole family is intimately familiar with every beam and stone and we have memories, some good, some not so good (miserably cold in the winter, for example, before the central heating went in), going right back over the twenty five years since we first started to come here. It is one of four houses right at the end of a lane. Two of the houses are in disrepair and uninhabited, owned by our neighbour Antoine who is rarely seen in a change of clothes and on hot days washes his feet in the duck pond. The house has views on one side over medieval St Puy and on the other over open farmland, woods, vineyards and hills. It is very quiet indeed and we expect only one car a day, the postwoman. The quality of the light, the clean air, the corners of the garden where you can see the view and house from various angles, hoopoes, redstarts and many other birds, insects and lizards, the bright green tree frogs, the dragonflies and bats, the smell of roses, jasmine, thyme and rosemary, the warm mellow old floor tiles, the honey-coloured stone, all combine to make it a very special place indeed. I thought some years ago of linking Winchester with our tiny hamlet by walking the whole distance and that by so doing the two places where we have spent so many happy years as a family might be drawn, as by an invisible thread, even closer together.

I am now out of the village on the narrow white stone track I know intimately that drops down towards the river Gèle, past the little house called Marin that is built on an outcrop of solid rock, past La Bourdette des Soldats, the farm that got its name during the 100 Years' War and in whose front garden is a 100 year-old tortoise, past Chatas with its ancient corner stone bearing the stone mason's mark (probably originally from the old chapel, now virtually disappeared, at the top of the next hill), on and up a gentle incline and then the final descent to our little hamlet with the shutters of our house looking bright and white just where the road peters out. The roses are dripping with flowers and hips; the clumps of late-flowering sedums are heavy with bees; the lizards rustle among the first fall of autumn leaves on the terrace; and the sun, finding a gap in the racing clouds, shines warmly on my return.

The following day my neighbour makes an observation of some depth, but I've heard it in different guises all along my route:

'Ça oui, il faut le faire, hein? C'est pas évident'.
'Fancy, all that way…that's quite something'.

Appendix 1

This is what I took with me:

- a back pack (you mustn't call it a haversack these days – far too old-fashioned) with two extra little pockets on the straps which were useful for things like money, knife, pen and camera;
- a very good quality pair of boots;
- 2 aluminium walking sticks (sorry, poles) to assist with walking and to provide some protection from angry dogs;
- waterproof trousers (a snip at £15-99 in Millets sale: 'Try the crouch test to see if they fit, sir', the idea no doubt being that if you can crouch in them you'll be able to lift your leg comfortably over gates and fences, provided you have the necessary suppleness in your lower limbs, which I have not – it was the most I could do simply to crouch whilst the supple shop assistant looked on smiling politely);
- a pair of flip-flops for evening wear weighing only a few grams;

- a change of clothing (three pairs of pants, three pairs of good proper walking socks, one pair of trousers, one pair of shorts, three 'microlite' very lightweight tee shirts);
- one thin fleece;
- one lightweight all-weather jacket;
- a one litre water bag;
- 5 small self-seal plastic bags to stow food;
- a thick wodge of plasters in case of blisters;
- a pack of antiseptic wipes;
- a small stiff-backed notebook and a fine nib pen;
- 30 Buzet wine labels to serve as writing paper;
- half a dozen nappy pins for suspending damp clothes on the outside of my back pack as I walked;
- a short length of stout string to serve as a washing line;
- washing powder (lighter than liquid) for clothes;
- electric razor, digital camera, mobile, all with chargers;
- nail scissors; toothbrush and toothpaste (no soap, shampoo or towel for I assumed these would be available when I stopped for the night);
- glasses with a cord round my neck and a spare pair just in case;
- five 1cm to 1km maps each weighing 100 grams and a clear plastic map holder for protection in bad weather; 3 large envelopes already stamped and addressed so I could send on the maps when I had finished with them;
- a sheet of A4 with travel insurance details; Health card; three credit cards; cheque book; passport;

- a pencil-thin torch;
- a good quality compass (vital);
- and most importantly two tiny thin slivers of flint broken loose by the winter frosts from the medieval wall surrounding Winchester Cathedral Close destined to be displayed somewhere in the French house if/when I made it.

These were all my possessions and they came to no more than seven and a half kilos, and some of them (razor, 'phone, camera), weren't really necessary at all.

Appendix 2

I contacted the Confraternity of St James in London in search of walking maps and suggestions of routes but, although very helpful, all their long-established medieval paths in the north were (surprisingly) not yet well signed and some tended (again surprisingly) to take somewhat circuitous routes so I had to make up my own. I decided to walk mainly on small roads and relatively straight footpaths so as to be able to get from A to B in as direct a way as possible. There are maps published in France (IGN: 1 cm to 1 km) which include most roads and footpaths. My route was quite simple. I drew a reasonably straight line on an average-sized map of France from St. Malo to St. Puy taking care to include all the large villages and small towns and then purchased all the local maps along the line. I marked out the straightest possible route on the local maps (swerving east just north of Bordeaux) with a marker pen, mainly along the smallest roads and tracks.

My walk from Winchester to St. Puy was 752 kilometres (470 miles) in all and in this figure I have included taking the odd wrong turning. I have not included the evening strolls taken around towns and villages after finishing my day's walk. The total number of days was thirty two of which four were rest days, so the average day's walk was just under 27 kilometres.

Winchester -	kms
• Bishop's Waltham	20
• Portsmouth	25

(one rest day crossing the Channel)

St. Malo -	
• Bois Mandé	34
• Hédé	23
• Rennes	27
• La Couyère	35
• Châteaubriant	28
• St. Mars la Jaille	30
• Ancenis	23

(one rest day)

• Beaupréau	30
• St. Laurent sur Sèvre	34
• Réaumur	33
• Foussais-Payré	28
• Niort	34

(One rest day)

• Aulnay	38
• Matha	19

•	Jarnac	26
•	Châteauneuf sur Charente	18
•	Lerse	20
•	Festalemps	33
•	St. Laurent des Hommes	24
	(One rest day)	
•	Le Fleix	27
•	Eymet	20
•	Puymiclan	29
•	Clairac	25
•	Bruch	23
•	Francescas	24
•	St. Puy	22
	Total:	**752 kms**

Acknowledgements

Very heartfelt thanks to you all for your encouragement, sage advice, practical help, memorable food and wine, and companionship at all stages in the preparation of this book: Rosie, Melissa and Tom, Edmund and Lindsey, Patrick; Arthur and Gabrielle Richardson; Hugh and Bernadette Taylor; David and Christine Hallah; Angela Thomas; Matthew and Marjorie Huntley; Nicky Wood; Adam Crick; David Lorimer; Carolyn Fairbairn; Simon Woolley; Alan Conn; Lachlan Mackinnon; Suzi Rae; Paddy and Wendy Sandford-Johnson; Patrick Kiely; David and Louise Woods; James Anderson; Lance Butler; James Webster; Michel Renouard; Didier and Sylvette Gefflaut.

Special thanks to Marion Robinson and her late husband Adam, and Richard and Anne Manley who all suggested I should walk for charity and who with characteristic kindness, generosity of spirit and unstinting effort went on to organise all the fund raising for neurological research.